Pauline Quirke began her career in television at just eight years old, appearing in *Dixon of Dock Green*. She went on to host children's TV series in the 1970s, before taking a role in *The Elephant Man*. In 1989 Pauline was cast as loveable loudmouth Sharon Theodopolopodous in *Birds of a Feather*, which turned her into a household name. She remained with the series until its conclusion in 1998 after over 100 episodes, before gaining critical acclaim for performances in *Down to Earth* and *The Sculptress*. After recent roles in *Skins*, *The Bill* and *Casualty*, in 2010 Pauline joined the cast of *Emmerdale* where she played the part of chirpy chatterbox Hazel Rhodes.

Where Have I Gone?

Pauline Quirke

CORGI BOOKS

TRANSWORLD PUBLISHERS
61–63 Uxbridge Road, London W5 5SA
A Random House Group Company
www.transworldbooks.co.uk

WHERE HAVE I GONE?
A CORGI BOOK: 9780552165648

First published in Great Britain
in 2012 by Bantam Press
an imprint of Transworld Publishers
Corgi edition published 2013

This book is substantially a work of non-fiction based on the life,
experiences and recollections of the author. In some limited cases names
of people, places, dates, sequences or the detail of events have been
changed solely to protect the privacy of others. The author has stated to
the publishers that, except in such minor respects not affecting the
substantial accuracy of the work, the contents of this book are true.

A CIP catalogue record for this book
is available from the British Library.

Addresses for Random House Group Ltd companies outside the UK
can be found at: www.randomhouse.co.uk
The Random House Group Ltd Reg. No. 954009

The Random House Group Limited supports The Forest Stewardship
Council® (FSC®), the leading international forest-certification organization.
Our books carrying the FSC label are printed on FSC®-certified paper. FSC
is the only forest-certification scheme endorsed by the leading environmental
organizations, including Greenpeace. Our paper-procurement
policy can be found at www.randomhouse.co.uk/environment

Typeset in 11.75/16pt Berling by Falcon Oast Graphic Art Ltd.
Printed and bound by CPI Group (UK) Ltd, Croydon, CR0 4YY.

2 4 6 8 10 9 7 5 3 1

For Hetty. For her love, wisdom,
strength and sense of humour.

Darklight

Contents

Acknowledgements

Thanks go to Terry for listening to my ramblings and making sense of them, and to Pat who thought this book would be a good idea. To Max and Jo Clifford for their friendship and encouragement, and to Gavin Blyth (RIP) who invited me to join the *Emmerdale* party.

To all the people who thought that the little freckled-faced chubby kid from Hackney had some talent, and to everyone who has watched a programme I've been in and enjoyed it. Thank you. x

Preface

I decided to write this book for one reason and one reason only – me! Why? Well, I'd reached a point in my life when something had to change, and fast. You might call it a crisis point; it certainly felt like one to me. There I was, a wife, mother and busy actress in my early fifties, tipping the scales at almost 20 stone and getting fatter by the day. I was tired, I was unhealthy, and I felt bloody miserable. What is it they say, the only way is up? Well, I guess that's what this book is all about: falling flat on your face . . . literally . . . and then getting up again!

When I first had the idea to write the book, full of enthusiasm, back in the summer of 2010, my plan was to present it in the style of a bright and breezy journal with a daily food diary included. I was just starting work on one of Britain's most popular television shows, *Emmerdale*; I'd had to move away from my family to live in Leeds, and I'd just made the momentous decision to lose a massive eight stone in weight – all at the same time. There was a lot going on, folks, and it was as exciting as it was terrifying. My big idea was to scrupulously document this voyage into the unknown: sharing my day-to-day life with you lovely readers along with my thoughts and fears – whilst charting my weight-loss journey with inspiring tales of triumph and, quite possibly, despair. I then intended to pepper the text with lots of witty but helpful dietary tips and healthy recipes that I'd gathered along the way, and by the end of the book I would be slim and glamorous and look exactly like Kate Moss, and it was all going to be fabulous. That was the plan, anyway.

Unfortunately, as you'll discover when you read on, my plan went somewhat awry and I was about as good at keeping a journal and a food diary as I was at sticking to the aforementioned diet. The whole thing went to pot, in fact. I ended up piling on even more weight, then I got fed up with keeping the diary, and suddenly it looked as though my wonderful notion of writing a book was doomed to complete failure. My husband, Steve, didn't agree at all.

'Surely this makes for an even more interesting story,' he argued, 'a more honest story? I think you should keep writing. Write about what happens when you fail. When you hit rock bottom and you have to face the world and start all over again.'

Seriously?

So that's exactly what I've done, and eventually *Where Have I Gone?* has evolved into so much more than just a journal. Yes, I've documented a rather tumultuous year, but quite apart from that I've remembered and recounted some funny, treasured (and some not quite so funny and not quite so treasured) memories, plus a fair few tales from my forty-year career as an actress into the bargain. I also found myself jotting down some of my own views on any number of subjects (never backward in coming forward), so you've that to look forward to as well.

It certainly has been a remarkable and sometimes rather bumpy journey but, when all's said and done, I've been extremely fortunate to have the family life and the varied career that I've had. All the things that have happened to me this year have made me think about exactly how I got to where I am . . . not to mention where I'm going next! And in the end I'm very glad I did write it all down, so that I'm able to share it with you, and get it all off my chest!

1
My Doomed Diet Diary
June 2010

Iwas a skinny child, a slim teenager, a curvy woman, and then a big woman. And according to my bathroom scales right now, damn them, I'm a very big woman. How the hell did that happen? Well, I guess I know how it happened.

Despite this somewhat alarming revelation, my husband, Steve, and my kids, Emily and Charlie, love me very much and will no doubt continue to do so; and I have had a long, and not unsuccessful, acting career for 41 years. Yes, I've been coming at you through your television sets for that long: doesn't time fly when you're having fun? This is no mean feat as far as I'm concerned, big or small, as so many actors seem to be out of work half the time, or 'resting' as we in the trade politely put it. In fact, my weight hasn't ever been a big issue (pardon the pun) as far as producers hiring me – or not hiring me – goes.

Still, the plain truth of the matter is that I am bored with being fat. There, I said it: the 'F' word. And let's not beat about the bush here, friends, the word *is* fat. I'm not big-boned or pleasantly plump or anything else for that matter. I'm just fat! It's not a particularly fun fact to contemplate either, I can tell you. I mean, I sometimes wish someone would suddenly reveal that I have some weird and wonderful medical condition that's making me this way, but that just isn't going to happen. And just in case there are any psychologists out there waiting in the wings to tell me that I have an unhealthy relationship with food because I came from a one-parent family or had a poor upbringing blah blah blah – please don't bother! That's just Freud egg and chips to me. I have managed to get this fat all by myself, basically, because I'm greedy. I eat and drink too much and I exercise too little, and that's about the sum of it. That's all you really need to know.

Firstly, I didn't put this weight on overnight, did I? No! It's taken fifty years to get this 'fuller figure', and at the end of the day I like me, I really do! I'd just like me more if there was less of me – do you know what I mean? Right now, in fact, I weigh almost twenty old-fashioned stones and I plan to lose eight and a half of them. Yes, there you go: the horrible truth is out . . . I'm carrying another whole person's worth of fat around with me – and I intend to get rid of it!

I firmly believe that the issue of weight is a relative one – I mean, whether you're a big old lump like me, or just half a stone overweight and feel uncomfortable, it's the same mountain you have to climb. It's just that my mountain happens to be of the Ben Nevis variety, that's all. So there will be no silly fad diet for me, and God there have been some, haven't there? I mean the maple syrup diet tops the lot, doesn't it? And cabbage soup – yuk! Why wasn't there ever a doughnut diet? I could have stuck to that one, no problem.

As I have never, ever exercised before, I am going to treat myself (not sure that 'treat' is the correct word here, to be honest – but you know what I mean) to a personal trainer. Now I know a personal trainer is not a luxury that everyone can afford, but quite frankly mine is costing about the same amount of money I might spend on a week's worth of takeaway Chicken

Chow Mein or Lamb Pasanda, so there you go. I feel this is a must as I don't really have the confidence to go to a gym, but, to be honest, given that exercise in general is an alien concept to me, how I'm going to get along with this venture is anybody's guess.

I'm also about to start filming on *Emmerdale*, which looks like it's going to be a really, really busy schedule, and all meticulously organized. On any given day at any given time there will be three film crews working, so I might be learning lines for one director on set in the studio one minute, only to be whisked off to the village to film for another director the next. So if I can manage to lose weight during a busy working week like that, and resist the waft of the on-set caterer's sausages, I really will feel I've achieved something. On top of all this, as I'm going to be living in Leeds on my own while I'm filming, I won't have the discipline of preparing and cooking meals for my family every night. This could turn out to be a help or a hindrance – I just don't know yet! In fact, I feel like I'm stepping into the unknown both personally and professionally right now: after all, I've never worked on a TV soap before, and I've certainly never lost eight stone.

Right now, I just have to take the first step. And the first, very important step (apart from admitting what a sad state I'm in) is just to stand still. Before I do anything else I'm going to stop putting on weight for a couple of weeks – even that'll be a bloody first! Then I'm planning on losing just two pounds a week – that's it, two itsy-bitsy pounds a week. Easy-peasy, no? OK, we'll see. Whatever happens, I want to think of this as being the start of something and not the end. So here goes!

Saturday 26 June 2010

So why have I decided to attempt this mammoth undertaking now, I hear you ask. Why have I decided to lose eight stone? Well, to be perfectly honest I'd completely lost track of how fat I'd become. Perhaps I'd just locked the depressing realization of it away in the dark recesses of a kitchen cupboard in a tightly sealed Tupperware container – I'm not too sure. It was only when I was at the airport with Steve and the kids recently, headed for my beloved Mallorca, that the truth of it came tumbling out to smack me in the mush, and boy did it hurt!

I was on my way across the tarmac towards the plane when the grim, familiar apprehension came over me, and I felt every bit of colour drain from my face. That question. The same one that I'd asked myself before boarding every plane on every holiday for the last few years: will the seatbelt go round me? Suddenly I wanted to kick myself. I mean, what was wrong with me? It's not as though I hadn't suffered this dread and panic before. It was as if I'd had this incredible amnesia: complete memory loss about being too fat for the seatbelt until I was actually walking across the tarmac and up the stairs to the plane. It was only then that I'd say to myself, you stupid bitch! You've had seven months since you last went through this terrible ordeal. Seven months to get the weight off since your last holiday, but you didn't. And *now* you're panicking about it . . . again!

As I walked down the aisle of the plane my mind started racing with ludicrous questions. What kind of aircraft was this? Was it a 737 or a 747? Doesn't one of them have larger seats? Aren't the seats by the window supposed to be bigger? I could feel Steve and my kids looking at me as I sat down, knowing what I was feeling and hurting for me as I tugged the seatbelt across my body and felt its metal buckle cutting into me.

'Don't look at me. Don't look at me,' I felt like shouting, but instead all I said inside was a little prayer that the damned thing would stretch all the way round me and click neatly and securely into place under all the blubber. It'll go on, I told myself. It *will* go on. But it didn't go on, not this time. So, as discreetly as I could, I summoned the petrifyingly thin air stewardess for some assistance.

'Could I have an extension belt, please?' I muttered, as shyly and quietly as I could.

It was the question I'd always dreaded having to ask.

'I'll see if I have one,' she replied kindly.

Now these extension belts are meant for toddlers or babies and they are invariably a garish orange, so discretion here wasn't really an option, and of course she had to stroll all the way to the front of the plane where the belts were stored to collect one. I could see her there, whispering to another stewardess, this one so thin you could see right through her, and I was dreading that they might have run out of belts because the toddlers and babies, who take priority, had selfishly used them all up. What then? Would fatties like me have to get off the bloody plane and take their suitcases full of chubby holiday clothes with them? I found myself looking around to see how many small children there were. Oh bugger! There were quite a few.

Surely they would have run out of extension belts. It's amazing the scenarios one's mind creates in a moment of stress, but, however funny they might be, this one was real. And right then and there it wasn't funny at all.

Suddenly, though, panic over: it turned out that there was one, very bright, almost fluorescent orange belt left. I hardly knew whether to laugh or cry. I imagined the announcement over the public address system: 'Seat 37A, your extension belt is on its way.' I saw the see-through stewardess making her way back towards me: that really, really long walk, all the way to row 37, brandishing the fluorescent orange belt aloft and checking row by row and seat by seat for a woman with a baby *sans* seatbelt. When she finally spotted me – not a toddler in sight – I saw pity in her eyes . . . and I wanted to die.

All the way to Mallorca I stared out of the window. I couldn't look at or speak to Steve and he didn't speak to me. I just fixed my gaze out of the window of that plane until my neck was sore. In truth, nobody else on the plane knew what was going on. Nobody cared. But I knew, and that was enough. I had to do something, and I had to do it soon. I really couldn't go through that pain and humiliation again and that's a good enough reason for anyone to lose weight, right?

Sunday 27 June 2010

My fatness comes with a fatigue that I'd dearly love to shed along with all these extra pounds. Yes, folks, I'm tired. Tired of not being able to find clothes that fit me; tired of sunbathing on a hotel balcony when I'm on holiday because I'm too self-conscious to sit around the pool in a swimming costume; and mostly, I'm tired of feeling tired . . . all the time. More important than all that even is the fact that I'm just not healthy: I had a disc removed in 1991 (probably because I was overweight), I had gestational diabetes in 1994 when I was pregnant with my son Charlie (probably because I was overweight), and I had to have a hip replacement in 2009 (probably because . . . yes, yes, you guessed it) and then earlier this year I had a fall which resulted in a fractured ankle that refused to heal properly (you know why). And all because the lady loves Milk Tray!

I think it's time I sorted myself out – don't you? And what better time than now, when I'm about to start a whole new phase in my life anyway, with a brand new job on one of Britain's most popular TV soaps? On the other hand maybe I should be settling into the job first before thinking about such a challenge. No. That would just be another excuse, wouldn't it? It's got to be right now ... next Wednesday. That's when I start filming.

Monday 28 June 2010

I'm excited. Nervous. Nervous and excited, I suppose. I'm finally taking all the *Emmerdale* scripts out of their envelopes and putting them into neat piles on the desk in the hotel bedroom. I've actually got the jitters just doing that, so Christ knows what I'll feel like when it comes to actually learning them. I suppose it's daft really, the length of time I've been at this game, but *Emmerdale* is a big deal: it's a British institution! I know, I'll have a shower to calm myself down: a nice long, hot shower. When I get to the bathroom, however, I'm faced with the revelation that my daughter Emily has toddled off with the last of the shampoo, so I'm reduced to washing my barnet with Fairy Liquid antibacterial with the fresh whiff of eucalyptus. Still, at least I'm sure to be germ-free for the rest of the day. Hang on, though. Isn't eucalyptus what pandas eat? Or is that bamboo? Either way I'd best be on my guard. The last thing I need today is to be set upon by Chi Chi or any of her lairy mates who might mistake me for a tasty snack trotting around Leeds town centre.

I've got to go out though. I'm off to the studio to get my eyebrows threaded. Not plucked, threaded, if you don't mind. Well, it worked for SuBo . . . apparently. But when I get there, the make-up people decide to go for gold and have a crack at my upper lip and chin too – they're having a field day. Still, when push comes to shove I decide that not starting off my time on *Emmerdale* looking like David Bellamy can only be a good thing.

Tuesday 29 June 2010

I was sent to have my hair cut and coloured today. What with all that threading yesterday and now the hair, they must have thought I really needed sorting out before I stepped in front of the nation, terrifying all and sundry with my thick eyebrows and dull, life-less hair.

I guess if they're doing their bit to make me at least semi-glamorous, then the least I can do is try my best to help the process along and stick to this diet, which starts tomorrow (yikes!). I've mentioned to Gavin Blyth, *Emmerdale*'s main producer, that I intend to shed a fair amount of weight over the next few months, but hopefully it won't make much difference to the viewers because the change will be fairly gradual, unlike the de-bushing of my eyebrows!

In other news, I've found a fantastic flat – it's a penthouse, actually (she says in a posh voice) – in a place called Clarence Dock, which overlooks the canal and is just five minutes from the studio. It's got two bedrooms – both en suite – and a lovely living room-cum-kitchen, with a balcony overlooking the water. The fact that it's got two bedrooms means that the kids will have somewhere to sleep when they come and visit me, which is great. The downside of this apartment, however, is that it's also perched above one of the finest curry restaurants in Leeds, Mumtaz. As I'm sure you can appreciate, this is not great for a woman who is about to start on a diet in an attempt to shed eight stone, especially when said woman is rather a big fan of curry. Still, they also have a shop attached and I've just nipped down to see what's on offer. You know, to get in a few bits and pieces. My diet isn't starting till tomorrow so I might as well go out with a bang, no? Anyway, I'm pleased to announce that they have a huge dessert selection so I've bought a big strawberry cheesecake. What? It can be one of my five a day! It's not very Indian, though, is it? I might go back for a curry later, just to be polite.

It's now about 7.30 and I've just sat down with the scripts to look over my very first scene: scene 6, episode 5681. Now I remember what it feels like to be a kid on your first day at school: butterflies and nausea all at the same time. My very first line as Hazel Rhodes is to be, 'Oh, this'll do for me it will, it's absolutely gorgeous round here.' It's quite exciting to be honest, sitting in my new flat by the water, learning lines and eating curry. Yes! So I got the curry. Have you got a problem with that? I told you, the diet starts tomorrow! The strangest part of all is that I've just watched *Emmerdale* on TV, and tomorrow I'm actually going to be there. It's weird.

Usually when I learn scripts for TV, I'm just concentrating on one. With the last series I worked on, the police drama *Missing*, we'd work on one episode at a time. On *Emmerdale*, though, as with most soaps, we'll always be working on about 12 different scripts with several different directors. All of them may require me at different times, so you have to work out which director you're with and which scenes you're doing each day. On top of this, each director has his own unit and crew. Some will be at the purpose-built *Emmerdale* village, which is out in the countryside, some will be at the studio, which is the Woolpack Inn interior, and it's my job to work out who I'm with and when I'm with them. And I have to make sure I'm learning the right lines from the right scripts for each day's filming. Confused? You will be. I know I am! Working out this schedule is like asking someone with dyslexia to read the *Oxford English Dictionary* and then learn it by heart. Luckily for me it all seems to be meticulously organized.

I'll have an early night tonight. I'm being picked up at 6.30 am. Wish me luck!

Wednesday 30 June 2010

No breakfast (naughty)

Lunch: Tesco fish and veg sushi (not usually a big fish fan but this was quite tasty)

Dinner: Salsa chicken with mixed salad and a strawberry yoghurt (not on the same plate!)

So, it's my first day of *Emmerdale*, and the first day

of my diet. I was picked up this morning on time and driven straight to the *Emmerdale* village, and believe me I wasn't disappointed in the least. It's absolutely beautiful. I actually shed a little tear when I saw the Woolpack Inn because *Emmerdale* was one of my mum's favourite programmes. She'd have been so proud to see me in it. Anyway, I go straight into make-up, and the girls there offer to get me breakfast. I'm too nervous to eat, though, and I certainly don't want to get into the habit of wolfing down bacon butties every morning before I go on set. I'll go for the healthy option tomorrow once my stomach has settled: fruit, cereal and yoghurt. That's me from now on!

I've made a decision not to tell anyone at work about my diet, or anyone else for that matter, apart from Steve and the kids. I can't face the thought of having to explain my food choices when I'm on the set or when I go out to eat in a restaurant, and have to sit there extolling the virtues of my beetroot salad while everyone else is filling up on Scotch eggs. Aside from that, people yapping on about what they can or can't eat and how many flippin' calories they've consumed is just plain boring, right? If nobody knows what I'm trying to achieve and I have a dietary slip-up (a fugitive pasty leaping recklessly off the buffet table and into my cakehole, for instance) then only I will know it! It would be just one slip-up and tomorrow is another day. Plus the fact that if you're not talking about food all the time, you're not thinking about it.

The days I don't see Prea (that's my new personal trainer, don't you know) I've decided that I still need to exercise: maybe a spot of vigorous dusting or a little boogie around the flat for ten minutes. I've also decided to be a bit more inventive with my diet meals than I have been in the past and to try to inject a few different colours and textures into them. So with this in mind I've bought a lovely tuna steak for tea, but as I take it out of the bag it smells of the sea. Is that a good thing or a bad thing? I can't remember. So into the bin it goes. I won't risk it. There are easier ways to lose weight than through a dose of raging salmonella, I feel.

Tuesday 6 July 2010
I've not had much time to write at all for the last few days. It's taken quite a lot of concentration getting used to this complicated schedule. Thank heavens for the helpful assistant directors, I say! I have to admit, with everything that's been going on

I haven't had that much time to think about food one way or the other, let alone keep my food diary updated. Basically, I'm trying to stick to salads for lunch and meat or fish and vegetables for dinner, so she's still on track, folks. Never fear!

It's completely uncharted territory for me at work. Everybody else knows each other and they all know how everything ticks, having worked together on the show, day in, day out, for such a long time. That being said, my first few days have been really lovely, if a little daunting.

I felt like I needed a buddy to show me the ropes, and luckily I had one in Suzanne Shaw, who's a friend of mine and already working on the show. In fact, I guess Suzanne is partly the reason I'm on *Emmerdale* now. When she first joined the cast, she would come over to my house and I'd help her run through her lines: she would do her character and I'd read everybody else, and I really liked what I was reading. I'd been watching the show off and on for a while anyway, as I'd been hearing great things about a fantastic young actor called Danny Miller, who plays Aaron Livesy, but once Suzanne joined I started watching more regularly. So when my agent called to say there was an offer on the table from the producers of *Emmerdale*, it just seemed like fate. I knew Suzanne was enjoying herself on the show so I thought, why not go and see what their plans for me are?

Anyway, Suzanne took me by the hand on those first few days and showed me what was what, and who was who, and where to get my pass, and all the other things I needed to know, which was a great help, I can tell you. But actually I've been bowled over at how incredibly helpful and welcoming all the cast and crew have been. I think it's a northern thing if you want the truth! People can't seem to do enough for you and it has made this first week much easier than it might have been. I suppose there was a bit of a buzz about me joining the cast beforehand, and Suzanne had mentioned how much people were looking forward to me coming (no pressure there then!). Still, it's great to be enjoying myself and getting to know a whole new crowd of lovely people. I really feel a part of it already.

I've hit it off with Lucy Pargeter, who plays Chastity Dingle, and Charley Webb, who plays Debbie Dingle, straight away because they've all been so incredibly welcoming. But I actually get on with everyone so far, cast and crew alike, which is really nice, but quite exhausting each day when you turn up for work because everybody – and I mean everybody – says good morning! From my first encounter with the security guard as I enter the building, to every single person I pass in the corridor: the wardrobe people, the make-up people, the cleaners, the assistant directors, the ladies in the canteen and everyone else in between.

'Good morning, Pauline.'

'Morning!'

'How are you today, Pauline?'

'I'm good, thanks, how are you?'

'Fine, thanks!'

I mean, down south if you walked up to someone you didn't know and said good morning they'd probably think you were going to assault them, but not here in Yorkshire.

'Morning!'

'Hello there!'

'Hi, Pauline!'

God almighty, by the time I get to my dressing room I need a lie-down! I do love it, though.

Thursday 15 July 2010

    Breakfast: Small orange juice, wholemeal
        toast, Special K

    Lunch: Cheese salad

Dinner: Chicken with broccoli, mangetout and carrots
2 glasses of wine (oops!)
Strawberry yoghurt
2 squares of chocolate (God, I needed them!)

Well, I'm finding the filming itself really satisfying. Now I've got over the worry about whether the other actors think I'm any good or not, which is natural on a new programme, I suppose, I'm up and running. I like the fast pace and I like being a team player. That's what *Emmerdale* is about, and I guess I've always preferred jobs where you feel part of a working team, rather than simply a lead or supporting actor.

My first time filming in the Woolpack was particularly exciting. Like the Queen Vic in *EastEnders* and the Rovers Return in *Coronation Street*, the Woolpack pub is a familiar setting that I'd grown up with, watching *Emmerdale Farm* with my dear mum. Today I had four scenes to film, all with Deena Payne, who plays Viv, and there was a lot of giggling. My character, Hazel, gave Viv a ridiculous makeover and one of my lines was: 'The last time I had a bouffant like that I was on my way to a Duran Duran concert.'

The thing about my character, Hazel, is that she doesn't stop talking and is constantly making wise-cracks. That's her thing – incessant gabbling. Consequently, I've often got reams and reams of lines to learn, while other people in the scene can't get a word in edgeways. The rest of the actors really look forward to being in a scene with Hazel because they'll have hardly any lines to learn. She's a great character, though: warm and sincere, and a very loving mum. I think that's what attracted me to the role, really. Hazel is someone I can genuinely identify with.

Now I've also been to my second training session with Prea, though I'm not quite sure why because the first one knocked me batty. When you weigh as much as I do, even a brisk walk – forget about running – is very hard, so until I lose a bit of flab I guess my body will be in for a few more shocks along the way. Today she made me walk up seven flights of stairs. It nearly killed me, but I did it. It is possible. All the way up, all I could think of was whether a tank of oxygen would be at the top waiting for me.

To be honest, I feel a tad embarrassed when Prea and me go out for our walks. Yes, we could just be two mates off out for a brisk walk together, but I don't like the idea that people may realize that she's a personal trainer and I'm her big challenge. Apart from people feeling sorry for me for being over-weight, I expect there'd be just as many folk feeling sympathy for Prea and muttering, 'Good luck with that one, love,' under their breath! No, I'm sticking with the two friends out for a bracing stroll scenario, thank you. Then I notice the huge lettering on the back of her jacket, which reads *PERSONAL TRAINER*. Oh well!

I've been invited to ITV's summer reception tomorrow, and I'm really looking forward to that. All the *Emmerdale* cast are invited, and the cast of *Coronation Street*. I wonder what food will be on offer, though. I bet the nibbles will be tempting, not to mention fattening, so I'd best go easy on them. Anyway, I'm wearing white trousers, and a white top with a beautiful green and turquoise jacket. The jacket is on loan from the *Emmerdale* costume department, so I'd best try not to slop anything down it, eh?

Monday 19 July 2010
So much for leaving that party early the other night: I got home at 2.15 am. Well, us old girls don't get

out much, do we? We have to grab every opportunity with both hands. I managed to say hello to some of the cast of *Coronation Street* including Michael Le Vell, Barbara Knox (who looked fantastic) and Jane Danson, but I was a bit overwhelmed, to be honest, so I hope I wasn't too giggly. Peter Fincham, who is head of ITV, gave a lovely speech praising all the actors and writers of both shows. I resisted quite a lot of the wonderful food on offer but was less successful resisting the wine, I'm afraid. Still, you can't have everything, can you?

Exercise-wise I've seen Prea again today. I've told her that I don't want to exercise outside any more because I feel self-conscious, so now I've become the loony in my apartment block doing my personal training in the downstairs reception area in front of all the security cameras. The security men must be having a right old hoot watching that! Prea, meanwhile, is still insisting that I haul myself up and down the seven flights of stairs to my apartment every day, even though I've tried to explain to her that the only way I'd ever normally walk down a flight of stairs would be if the building was on fire or if there was a burger restaurant in the basement and the lift was broken. The woman seems to be armed to the teeth with all manner of torturous apparatus, which she has 'kindly' provided me with to use at my leisure: weights, and a medicine ball (although I'm not sure why it's called that as I certainly didn't feel any better after using it for ten minutes). I'm not sure about this exercise lark, to be honest. I feel dead after about five minutes and wonder how on earth I'm going to get through the next fifty-five. When people rave on at me about how much they love the gym, I just think . . . you're weird, you are!

I'm really missing Steve and the kids too, and it's quite tough getting used to walking into an empty flat every evening. Usually when I'm filming something I'm in every scene, so my working day would be 7 am till 8 pm, and if I'm not working I'll be shopping or cleaning or ferrying the kids back and forth, so it's more than just a little strange coming home and cooking for one. Still, it's making the dieting easier, so that's something. If I do ever feel the need to start snacking after dinner I just take myself off to bed. You're not hungry when you're asleep, are you? And as far as I know I've never actually eaten anything whilst sleeping. Of course, there is always the possibility that I could sleepwalk myself downstairs to the Indian restaurant and wake up to find I've ordered the set meal for one.

Wednesday 21 July 2010

Breakfast: Orange juice, toast, mixed fruit

Lunch: (*Emmerdale* canteen) Chicken salad with coleslaw (don't look at me like that – it was dry!)

Jacket potato with no butter (that was hard)

Dinner: Grilled pork chop, mushroom and asparagus (actually there were two pork chops, but they do come in packs of two!)

Banana (whoop de doo!)

A couple of glasses of wine

I'm so enjoying my new job! Do you know, up in Yorkshire they actually have a tea break in the morning, and then another in the afternoon? How very civilized! I haven't stopped for a tea break on a television programme for God knows how many years. Of course, this gives me plenty of time to chat and get to know people on the set, and to hear all about their families and tell them about mine, which is rather nice. The cast all know that I'm based down south and living on my own up here, so I'm always included in any social gathering. I've been made to feel part of the gang, so to speak. The only things I won't let anyone talk about around me, however, are the scenes and storylines that I'm not actually involved in.

'SHH! SHH! Don't tell me what's going on,' I'll shout if someone starts talking about a future plotline. 'I don't wanna know. I want to watch it on the telly. Take it outside!'

It's because I love good acting and good writing, and I'm a fan! I want to enjoy watching *Emmerdale* at home as well as being in it.

Talking of good actors, yesterday I had my first scene with Patrick Mower, who plays Rodney, and he is everything I hoped he would be: a lovely actor, and a complete and utter gentleman. I'm not sure how old he is but he's incredibly suave and a proper charmer. He's also very handsome, and when he kissed my hand after we'd finished the scene I think I may have giggled – just a little bit.

In other news, I went to Argos earlier and got myself a set of bathroom scales, as up till now I've been weighing myself on the Wii-fit. This does not seem to be accurate, in all honesty: it told me that on my first week of dieting I'd lost 4lb, then on the second week, 3lb (hurrah!). Last week it said I hadn't lost any, and then yesterday it said I'd lost

1 stone 5lb. Now I know that can't be right. I've been good, but not that flippin' good. So, much as I'd love to believe the latest of my Wii-fit's random weight calculations, I really can't – hence the scales. Right. Here goes. 19 stone 10? What? Oh Jesus, I think I'll go back to the lying Wii-fit.

Thursday 22 July 2010

So, the great bathroom scales debate rages on. I got on them this morning and they said 19 stone 4, so basically I've lost 6lb overnight. That's it! I just need to sleep more. Sleep yourself thin with Pauline Quirke! I make Prea get on them and they tell her that she's 7 stone 8, which is 6lb heavier than she really is. I'm confused. To be honest, I'm in a state of shock due to the fact that Prea actually weighs less than I want to lose. Now there's a sobering thought. Before this moment I'd just thought of it as losing x bags of sugar, but the stark realization that I've got to shed a whole person in weight is a kick in the teeth, to say the least. It suddenly dawns on me just how long and how hard this process might be, no, *will* be. It's pretty terrifying, and I'm ashamed to say that whether the bathroom scales were correct last night or this morning, I had no idea that I was headed for twenty stone. *Twenty stone*.

Right, I need to think about something more cheery. Someone at the studio got stung by a wasp today.

Sunday 1 August 2010

I guess you could say there's been a bit of a down-turn diet-wise in the last few days but there always seems to be a good excuse – well, I always seem to be able to find one when push comes to shove. Last Tuesday, for instance, was my first day off so I took my daughter, Emily, and Corey, who is Suzanne Shaw's little boy, to Whitby. I'd been told it was lovely there and well worth a visit so off we went. It took us two hours to get there, and by the time we got out of the car Corey was very grey indeed. Still, after he'd thrown his guts up in the car park he felt a lot better and we cheered him up by buying him a bucket and spade so he could play on the beach.

Then we fell upon a rather nice restaurant called Trenchers for lunch and I decided that I hadn't driven two hours just to pick at a flamin' salad, so I kicked off with a prawn cocktail and then dove straight into the haddock and chips. Gorgeous.

OK, so there's not much point in calorie counting today, but I don't care. It was worth it! And besides, I wouldn't have wanted to offend the good people of Whitby by not trying their fish and chips. It wouldn't have felt right. See what I mean about excuses?

Yesterday morning I drove home from Leeds to Beaconsfield and it took nearly four hours because of an accident on the M1. Still, rather than get the hump about being stuck in a traffic jam I thought about the poor sods in the accident who might not get home at all. Anyway, I'd just about got in the front door when we had to dash out again. My son Charlie was playing for the Showbiz Eleven in a charity football match at Oxford United. The singer Jess Conrad, who organizes these charity events, asked me if I would kick the first ball, which would have been a lot more fun if I hadn't been wearing open-toed sandals. Still, the game was great and Charlie scored a goal so we all came away happy. I had to dash off *again*, though, to Bristol for a dinner in aid of the Prince's Trust, and, of course, the menu was rather enticing. Yes, once again I was looking for excuses: I'd been dashing around; I was at a charity dinner. You guessed it. I ploughed my way right through that tantalizing spread as if I didn't have a worry in the world. I think I'd best stay away from those evil bathroom scales for a few days, eh?

And that was the last entry in my diary full of good intentions, folks: 'tis sad but true! After that I actually started to put on weight rather than losing it, and, of course, the last thing I wanted to do was document that sad fact. I felt like a failure. So what happened next, I hear you ask? What indeed . . .

2

A Christmas Break

Once you've mucked up at breakfast time there really is no going back. Well, that's what I would tell myself anyway. You just think, well, I've mucked up today already so I might as well carry on mucking up. And so this was how my so-called diet went on for me. Once I'd slipped up and had that juicy bacon roll from the *Emmerdale* canteen at breakfast, there really didn't seem any point in getting back on track for the rest of the day. I'd go back on my diet tomorrow. Sound familiar? Pretty soon, what had been an occasional 'treat' – i.e., the bacon roll – stopped being occasional. It became the norm. Still, though, I would find myself getting frustrated and wondering why I wasn't a dead ringer for one of Girls Aloud by now, after all my hard work and dedication. Of course, it never crossed my mind that it was my fault.

'Why haven't I been losing any weight?' I'd moan to Steve and myself. 'I've been so good. I've been working so hard and sticking to my diet. Why isn't it coming off me?'

But had I been good? For a start, with the *Emmerdale* schedule being what it was, I just couldn't seem to find the time to see Prea for training; in fact, what with the long filming hours and mammoth amount of line learning I didn't have the energy, let alone the time. When I looked back at the food I'd been eating during those weeks, I realized I hadn't done too well there either. Yes, I'd had a salad from the salad bar last Thursday, but the salad had included a great big pile of grated cheese. A little bit of quiche: that won't hurt, will it? I'd reason with myself. A bit of coleslaw 'cause it's a bit dry. And I was still buying clothes that were more or less as big as you can get from some of the 'larger ladies' fashion brands. The whole thing was starting to make me feel miserable. So what would I do? I'd have something nice to eat to cheer myself up. Classic! Good idea, girl!

'I deserve it,' I'd say, 'it's a treat.'

But what I really needed to do was face facts: after several weeks of dieting I had to admit that I'd just been kidding myself. I really didn't need Miss Marple to deduce what was going wrong, did I? No. It wasn't the bathroom scales that were broken – it was me. Along with the diary going out of the window big time, so did my resolve to shed the pounds. When autumn turned into winter it was even worse: I stopped 'being good' altogether, in fact I more than stopped being good. I went so far back down the wrong road – what with sausage and bacon baps in the morning and cheeseboards after dinner – that I began to put on even more weight.

'But it's cold, Pauline,' I'd tell myself. 'You deserve a hot meal. You've been working so hard, Pauline.'

The enticing options at the *Emmerdale* canteen would often be delicious meat pies, roast potatoes and the like: gorgeous, comforting, warming foods, princely portions invariably smothered in gravy (and this meant an extra bread roll at the end to mop it all up with). As far as I was concerned I deserved that sort of sustenance. After all, I'd been up since six filming in the freezing cold – so why not? Why not indeed? Then, as Christmas approached, disaster struck after a night out.

It had been a truly lovely evening at a restaurant

with a fair few of the *Emmerdale* cast and crew: a beautiful meal, plenty of wine. I have to say the folk at *Emmerdale* are very good at organizing lots of fantastic social events and get-togethers. One of the actors will say, 'Who fancies a night out on Saturday?' And off we'll go. It really is like a family affair.

Anyway, I digress. There had been a crowd of about thirty or forty of us, all celebrating the fact that we were breaking up for the Christmas holidays. I'd had a great laugh and a good drink, and I was very much looking forward to getting back home to the family in Beaconsfield. Now, as I'm sure many of you will remember, there'd been an awful lot of snow and ice that month, and as I got out of the cab outside my flat I caught my Ugg boot on the kerb and fell over. No big deal, you might think, and yes, I've certainly fallen over before and it wasn't the Ugg boot's fault. It was how I fell that was the problem: with a handbag, plus a bag of Christmas shopping weighing down my right arm. I twisted on to my side, bringing all my body weight down on my left arm as I crashed to the pavement.

I must have passed out at that point because the next thing I remember was the blurry vision of two young lads looming over me, asking if I needed help.

I was lying on the ground looking up at them with my left arm completely squashed underneath me.

'No, I'm all right,' I heard myself saying. 'I haven't broken it because I can still move my hand. I'm fine, I'm fine.'

When I tried to get up, though, I failed miserably and blacked out again. The next thing I knew there was an ambulance on the scene and I was being lifted into it. 'I haven't broken it,' I kept assuring the paramedics. 'I can move my hand.'

I was still holding on to the myth that if you can move something it isn't broken. Not so!

When I arrived at the hospital, in a real blur by this time, I had a cast put on and was moved into a room to recover. It wasn't an actual ward I was in but some sort of transitional room, but to be honest I could have been in the kitchen or the broom cupboard for all I knew, as I was drifting in and out of consciousness and there were comings and goings that I was only barely aware of. It hurt, though. Boy, did it hurt! I'd never broken a bone before and let me tell you I was in agony. But that was only part of it. I also had to face up to the glaring possibility that if I hadn't had 19 stone crashing down on my arm I might well not have shattered it. Who's to say? It certainly can't have helped. All in all, it wasn't the most agreeable fashion in which to commence my much anticipated Yuletide holiday, folks. Yay, Pauline! Happy Christmas.

It didn't end there either. Steve came up to Leeds to collect me and was an absolute godsend all weekend once we got back home. Still, I was in acute pain despite being on morphine, Tramadol and whatever super-strong pain relief the doctors had prescribed me.

'This is a pain beyond just breaking a limb,' I kept whining to my attentive hubby. 'There's something not right.'

By Monday I could bear it no longer and off we went to Stoke Mandeville Hospital to get it checked over. It turned out that the doctors who had originally treated me had forgotten to put a buffer between the cast (or pot, as they call it in Yorkshire) and my skin, and when the staff at Stoke Mandeville removed said pot, my poor arm had been ripped to pieces. It was in a terrible state, as if I'd had a razor blade rubbing against my skin, and I couldn't bear to look at it. It was that pain that I'd been enduring, not the break itself.

The next six weeks were a struggle, to say the least. During the two-week Christmas holiday, Steve looked after me fantastically and did everything for me, right down to cutting up my food. I couldn't have coped without him. I do have to say, however, that having your partner wash all your intimate bits and pieces is not as romantic as you might imagine, for either party. I managed to get through Christmas somehow: opening presents and cooking included. I did a full Christmas dinner for everyone, with a lot of delegating, mind you, but at least my right arm was working so I could get stuff in and out of the oven well enough. There was the small matter of a batch of cauliflower cheese clattering to the floor at one point, but what the family didn't know wouldn't hurt them as far as I was concerned, so back in the pot that went and no one was any the wiser.

Once I was back at work after the holiday, and coping more or less on my own, I found myself getting rather intimate with the ladies in the costume department – well, you do when you have to ask someone to hoist your bra on for you every morning, don't you? And then I was straight back into filming, broken arm or not. I wasn't even able to dose myself up with strong painkillers while I was filming, in case I looked too spaced out on screen or couldn't remember my lines – can you imagine?

'Oh look at Pauline Quirke, she's off her head in the Woolpack, poor love!'

So I had to put up with a lot more discomfort than I had done over the holiday, whether I liked it or not. The funny thing is that my injury wasn't even written into the script at first, so there are quite a few scenes with me looking like Clint Eastwood in *A Fistful of Dollars*, with ponchos and bloody great shawls wrapped round me to cover it up. Apparently Twitter was abuzz with speculation as to why Pauline Quirke was semi-armless in every scene. One bright spark even suggested that I was wearing a cast for effect. What, like a fashion accessory? Of course, darling, everyone's wearing a pot this season, don't you know? I'm laughing about it now, but at the time I was pretty near rock bottom.

One morning, Lucy Pargeter offered to get my shopping for me, knowing how difficult things were. I was so touched: it's this kind of help that will ultimately get me through, I thought. I had to keep working after all; I couldn't just say to the producers, 'Excuse me, can we kindly stop filming till my arm gets better, please?'

There was one particular morning when I felt really down, though, struggling to wash myself in the shower.

'It's just an inconvenience, Pauline,' I tried telling myself. 'Some people have to put up with this sort of thing all their lives.'

It didn't help. What with the constant pain and the ham-fisted inelegance of trying to do the simplest of day-to-day chores with only one hand, there was the nagging voice inside that kept telling me that if I hadn't been as big as I was, it might not have ended up like it did. I'd spent years in denial about the connection between my health and my weight. I remember how stroppy I used to get with the doctors every time they mentioned it. To me it seemed like any time I was in the surgery for any-thing – even an earache – doctors would connect it with how fat I was, and so I ended up blotting it out. Even when, back in 2009, I'd been shown an X-ray of the damage to my right hip, worn away by the amount of weight it was carrying – even when I could hear my knees creaking as I went up the stairs because they were under so much strain – I was still secretly telling myself it wasn't because I was fat. After all, the left hip was fine and dandy and that was carrying the same amount of weight, wasn't it? Denial all the way!

Breaking my arm and the ensuing pain and in-convenience, however, had finally brought the reality of it into sharp focus. It became an ugly reminder of how everything I'd planned only a few months before had not just fallen by the wayside, but crashed into a flaming great chasm – the diet, my food diary, the training, my goal to get fitter and my plans for a new me. There was no kebab or cheeseburger in the world that could have made things better at that point.

3

Drastic Action Required

I am a strong person: I truly believe that. But when I look back at how I was feeling during winter 2010, it was like all the fight had gone out of me. When I'd started on *Emmerdale* I really had wanted to change things about myself: the way I looked, how I ate and my relationship with food generally. Gradually, though, the combination of being away from my family for long periods, arduous workdays, and the pain of breaking my arm and then getting through Christmas had worn me down and I had to admit defeat. From the moment I first got on those wicked bathroom scales six months earlier, imagining that I might be a hefty 17 stone, which would be bad enough, and finding out it was more like 19, the rot had started to set in. I was completely rubbish at point counting, and calorie counting, and weighing food and being strict with myself; plus I hadn't felt like I'd had the time or the motivation for training sessions with Prea.

How big do you have to get, though, before you decide to turn it around? On New Year's Day 2011, I finally dared to get back on the scales and I was 19 stone 6lb. Crikey, how had that happened? A couple of weeks before, I'd watched a programme with the kids that included an item about a famous sumo wrestler who tipped the scales at 20 stone. So I was, in fact, just a few pounds lighter than a sumo wrestler. Now there's an image that doesn't make you feel terribly attractive or alluring, let me tell you. *That's* how big you have to get!

The scary thing was that while I was up in Leeds before Christmas I hadn't been losing weight or even staying the same. I'd actually been getting bigger, and when I look back at it now I can see that most of the time I was eating out of plain, old-fashioned boredom. It wasn't as if I was hungry – I couldn't even remember what it was like to feel hungry. In fact I don't think I'd been hungry for thirty years because I'd never leave enough time between meals and snacks to let that happen. I wasn't sure where it would all end, but what I did know was that I wasn't going to lose weight just by talking about it; I was fed up with listening to myself. It was a case of 'Either do something about it, Pauline, or shut up and stay fat.' I needed to take some drastic action. What's that old adage? What doesn't kill you makes you stronger. Well, I finally saw a lifeline, and I grabbed it.

A company called LighterLife had approached me a few weeks previously about trying their weight-loss plan and doing some publicity for them along the way. The company would provide me with everything I needed, food and sustenance-wise, plus a counsellor who I'd be in constant contact with, and who would keep a record of my weight loss with regular weigh-ins. My side of the bargain would be to lose a substantial amount of weight and therefore, by being in the public eye, to help demonstrate the success of the plan. I'd also be expected to take part in weekly group meetings with other people on the plan, and learn about the philosophy behind the diet, which would hopefully help me keep the weight off once I'd lost it.

In layman's terms, LighterLife is a food replacement programme where normal meals are substituted with very low calorie packs that you mix with hot or cold water. There's a shepherd's pie, a chilli con carne, porridge, various soups and shakes, even chocolate snack bars; but everything is very low calorie and you only have the prescribed amount each day and nothing more. The packs contain all the nutrients your body needs, so it's not unhealthy, but it's certainly drastic. For someone like me, with more than three stone to lose (although I was looking to lose considerably more than that!), the prescribed programme is called 'total', which means complete abstinence from any other food apart from the four LighterLife packs a day. Nothing else. Zero! The idea is that you won't feel hungry – though perhaps a little light-headed after a couple of days – and then after three or four days you will go into ketosis, which is when your body starts to burn all the surplus fat it has stored, which in my case was eight and a half stone. I was made aware that there was no grey area as far as I was concerned: even the sugar in one biscuit could kick me off the ketosis and therefore hamper any progress I was making. I had to be unwaveringly dedicated if I was going to achieve my goal.

Now, I have to be honest and say that the LighterLife plan that I was about to undertake is not for the faint-hearted. Apart from the food abstinence, I was only allowed black tea or black coffee, or water. No booze, no diet drinks and no fruit juice. Just four little food packs a day. Yikes! It was going to be tough, especially when there were parties and social events to contend with. Even a simple dinner at a restaurant with the family was going to be problematic.

I had to ask myself how badly I wanted it. Was I prepared to make such a big commitment in order to change my life? Give up, at least for a while, one of my favourite things in the world – grub? I'm pleased to announce that the answer was a great, booming 'YES!'

When you start a drastic weight-loss plan like this, you really do need to take advice from a doctor – in fact, LighterLife insist on it. So off I toddled to my GP for a full going-over to make sure I wasn't about to do myself any damage, and that my body could cope with such a radical, and hopefully speedy, change. After all, I'd had my fair share of health problems: I wanted to make sure there were no more hidden ones ready to jump out and bite me on the bum while I was doing a full-on diet. Plus, and I guess this goes without saying, LighterLife, as a company, aren't particularly keen on the idea of people dropping dead whilst following their regime.

Apart from the initial medical, LighterLife also insist that you have a monthly blood pressure and pulse reading, which you can get done at a pharmacy, just to make sure you're ticking along nicely as you shed the pounds. For me it was a no-brainer: I mean, how could losing weight like this be any more dangerous than staying as fat as I'd become? Surely that was more likely to kill me than a strictly regulated diet.

Once I'd been OK'd by my GP, I decided to dive straight in with the eating plan on 3 January when *Emmerdale* began shooting again, and I won't pretend I wasn't terrified: terrified of failing, terrified of being hungry, and terrified of letting down the company who were sponsoring me. However, there have been many times in my life when I've been absolutely petrified of doing things and I've always got through them. In fact, I've spent most of my working life feeling scared to varying degrees. I went through 101 episodes of *Birds of a Feather* not sleeping the night before filming them and vomiting before the actual taping: the lines going round and round in my head all night, then the torturous twelve-hour build-up on the actual day with a feeling of doom and a dreadful knot in my stomach. There was also the time when Linda

Robson and I did our first ever TV chat show interview – on the Terry Wogan show. We were both petrified that evening.

Nothing, though, has ever come close to the paralysing fear I had during the filming of a series called *Jobs for the Girls*, in which Linda and I had to learn what it takes to succeed in a variety of challenging professions. One of these was to train as a classical opera singer, and, alongside soprano Lesley Garrett, perform 'Rule Britannia' at a concert at Kenwood House in north London with a full symphony orchestra and in front of 9,000 music lovers. Now *that* was terrifying. In fact, at the time I was very pregnant with Charlie and I remember praying that I would go into labour early, just so I could get out of the dreadful ordeal. Once I realized that wasn't going to happen, I tossed around the idea of throwing myself in front of a bus – anything to worm out of getting up on that stage in a posh frock in front of all those people and making a complete idiot of myself. It didn't help matters that we'd had to arrive at Kenwood House for rehearsals at 9 am, a full twelve hours before we actually had to get up on stage to perform. It was like being called to the dentist's waiting room two days before you're due to have your tooth taken out!

As you've probably all gathered, however, I didn't actually throw myself under a bus. Yes, there were a few titters from the audience as we walked on but that's hardly surprising, is it? I mean, first they see Lesley Garrett – one of the country's greatest sopranos – striding confidently on to the stage, and then they clock us two old tarts shuffling on behind her. It must have been quite a sight; not what they were expecting at all. Still, I got through it. You do, don't you? You get through it. In fact, not only did I get through the performance at Kenwood House but I thoroughly enjoyed it, too; and once I got off stage I wanted to do it all over again. I was actually quite angry with myself for worrying so much, plus I'd lost a whole night's sleep fretting about it.

So as far as I was concerned this eating plan, however drastic, was going to be no different. Yes, it scared me, but the outcome just might be fantastic. So I was simply going to do it one step at a time. Every journey starts with one step, right? I even marked out an imaginary journey across my kitchen floor in Leeds. Losing eight and a half stone was going to be like walking from one side of the room to the other, and I have to say, on that first day it looked a long way across that kitchen floor.

One of the things that helped spur me on, though, apart from wanting to shed the weight, was the sense of responsibility I felt to LighterLife. Something that Steve and I have always instilled in the kids, right from when they were little and had pet hamsters and the like, is that if you take on a commitment you have to stick with it. That's how I felt about this weight-loss plan, however terrifying it seemed on day one. There was a firm commitment, a contract in fact, and once the news of what I was undertaking was out there, I also knew that people were going to be watching me. I didn't want to let those people down either. I wanted people to be watching me on *Emmerdale* and saying, 'She's getting smaller; she's looking better.' I wanted that more than anything. I liked the idea that some woman somewhere who was having a hard time losing weight might see me getting thinner on TV and think, 'I can do that!'

These scenarios were some of the tools I used to help me overcome my fear. Of course, there was also the possibility that if I did slip up while I was under contract, some smart Alec paparazzi type would snap an unbecoming picture of me sneaking out of Greggs with a half-eaten cheese and onion pasty about my person – not a good look! So that was another concern. The main thing, however, was always me and how I felt about myself, and how desperately I wanted to face those feelings head on. I knew that I was only going to do this once, and I knew that it had to be now. No slip-ups this time. I was up for it!

So how was this going to work day to day? I decided that I would keep the whole thing under wraps for the first month, just to see how I got on. I also decided that, at least for a while, I wasn't going to tell any of my friends or work colleagues about LighterLife. I had no desire to be eating my packs in the canteen in front of the cast, or boiling up the kettle ready to add hot water to my shepherd's pie or chilli con carne for all and sundry to see. I was just going to get on with it. I was sure people would be too busy eating their own lunches to fret about why Pauline Quirke wasn't skulking around clutching a tuna and sweetcorn baguette, or tucking into a meat and potato pie covered in HP sauce, but I didn't want to have to explain myself to anyone who came up and quizzed me about what I was eating. Plus it's boring talking about what you can't eat. I've come across so many people on various weight-loss plans over the years, and it soon becomes their sole topic of conversation: what they've eaten or what they're not allowed to eat but would dearly love to. This was *my* thing and talking about it wasn't going to make it any easier.

So in those first few weeks, when it was time to eat, I would just take myself off to my dressing room, make my pack, and then go back to work when I'd finished it. That was the plan. I decided not to tell even the producers of *Emmerdale* about the diet. I knew that their only concerns would be about continuity: say, for instance, if Hazel were to walk into the Woolpack one day weighing 19 stone 6, and then come back the next day looking like Twiggy. Well, that certainly wasn't going to happen with the speed at which we filmed *Emmerdale*. No, it would be a gradual weight change, so I just kept it buttoned and told no one.

I was also determined not to draw attention to it when I was out in restaurants with the family. I didn't want to stop going out for family celebrations and special occasions, but by the same token I certainly wasn't going to ask the nearest waiter to scuttle off to the kitchen to make up one of my packs for me while everyone else was perusing the menu. To me that would be making a hoo-ha out of it and I definitely didn't want that. No, I'd either eat my pack before we went out, or look forward to it when we got home. Simple. Or at least I hoped it would be.

As I said before, I'd decided to start this new regime on the morning of 3 January 2011. Well, you should have seen me on the night of 2 January! You've never seen anything like it. Emily was staying with me at the flat in Leeds and we went all out. I opened a bottle of Viña Sol, I made a trip downstairs to Mumtaz and tucked into one of their delicious, charcoal-grilled chicken tikka kebabs – there was no stopping me. I couldn't get it all down me fast enough! It was a last gasp, so to speak. But when I woke up on the morning of 3 January that was it. I'd made a commitment, not only to LighterLife and myself, but also to all the fat men and women out there who I was supposedly going to inspire. There was no turning back.

4

Last of the Pit Stop Pasties

I'd like to share with you a little theory I have about motorway service stations. You see, when you're driving back and forth between London and Leeds as much as I found myself doing, you find yourself in a fair few of them: stopping for a wee, or a bit of sustenance for the trip, to put petrol in the car, or just to break up the long journey. From my house to *Emmerdale*, as it were, is 198 miles, and I always stopped once on the journey going north or south at one of these weird and wonderful oases, varying the location from time to time.

As the weeks went by I became quite fascinated to see if one motorway service station was different from another: did some of them, perhaps, have a more upmarket sort of clientele, or was there a more varied selection of products on offer at certain locations? Anything to break the monotony of my journey was a bonus as far as I was concerned. Unfortunately, in the not too distant past, this pit stop would have involved eating, and a pasty of some sort would invariably have found its way into my hot little hands. Failing that it might have been a cheese baguette, or a packet of cheese and onion crisps, or a cup of tea . . . or all of the above! In fact, for the first six months working on *Emmerdale* (especially after the 'diet' had gone to pot) I, Pauline Quirke, was doing my bit – just like Heston Blumenthal before me – to test out the varied fare on offer at the service stations of the M1 for the nation's benefit.

So, to return to my theory: I truly believe that some people actually go to motorway service stations for their holidays. It's true! It's a fact, I'm telling you. I mean, if you're going to stop at one of those places, what do you do? You get out of your car, you get petrol, eat something, go for a wee, and then you get back in your car and pootle off, right? There's a reason to be there, so people should be walking like there is a sense of purpose about what they are there to achieve, right? Wrong! In my experience of motorway service stations, there are far too many people in shorts, sandals and sun-tops wandering aimlessly in and out of the shops and restaurants browsing – as if they're in some sort of Spanish marketplace. I've seen families laughing and sitting on the grass with picnic hampers and rugs. Why would you do that? Sure, if you have a hankering to ingest more fuel and fumes than your body could ever cope with, then fine, but otherwise . . . WHY? Still, there these happy campers are: with their little children, with their pets, having a nice picnic lunch. So I can only surmise that these people have forgone the Thomson's holiday package or Center Parcs this year and have instead plumped for a mini-break at a service station. 'Ooh, we're 'avin' the last week of August, first week of September this year . . . Watford Gap!'

From 3 January 2011, however, my service station stops were going to be less and less frequent. Perhaps I'd stop for a cup of black coffee or a wee, but that would be it. No more pasties and no more crisps. This was serious. Time to get real. When I opened that first LighterLife pack of porridge on the morning of the 3rd and poured the hot water on, it really hit me how long a journey I had in front of me. After all, it wasn't something I was going to be doing for a couple of weeks, or even a couple of months: this was it. For the foreseeable future, all my sustenance would be coming out of these little packs and I had to get used to that fact, fast. It also wasn't something I was just doing till I'd lost a little bit of weight either, nor was it just to give me a kick-start. I was in this until I was a healthy size, which for me meant dropping eight and a half stone.

Halfway through the first week everything seemed pretty much hunky-dory. I wasn't craving anything I shouldn't be, my teeth were still there and my hair was still there. So far so good! By the end of the first week, I was really looking forward to my weigh-in. Surely I'd lost loads. I'd been told to expect a good result the first week, so I had high hopes. When I discovered I'd actually lost 10lb after one week I knew I'd done the right thing. I knew that even though the results wouldn't be as dramatic every week, this was the best way for me to do it. Not the best way for everyone perhaps – but for me. I didn't have to negotiate food colour-codes and calories or worry about what to put in my shopping basket and what to leave on the shelf, and I didn't have the opportunity to play fast and loose with the salad bar options in the *Emmerdale* canteen. That suited me fine. All that choice malarkey would come up again, once I'd reached my target weight of 11 stone. But for now, I was just happy going to bed every night and telling myself: Well done you! You got through another day.

Now together with the packs and the snack bars, there is also a whole philosophy concerning cognitive behaviour that goes along with the programme. This was something else I would have to get my head around. Why had I developed the bad eating habits that I had over the years? Why did I eat more than I needed to? And how was I going to change that behaviour when and if I reached my target weight and size? I know, it all sounds a bit like a typical bloomin' self-help manual, doesn't it? Well, unfortunately for those of us of a more substantial framework, if we don't tackle the root cause we're likely to just pile the pounds back on the minute we ditch the diet and catch sight of an Angus Steakhouse.

Every week while you're on the plan, you have to take part in a counselling session with a group of people who are also doing LighterLife: a bit like a WeightWatchers meeting, I suppose. It really is a great chance to talk about how you're getting on, how much weight you have or haven't lost, and to hear how other people are coping with such a strict regime. These sessions, every Monday night at eight, are especially useful for anyone who may be feeling like giving up or be having a weak moment or a craving for food they shouldn't be eating. Hearing words of encouragement from others in the same boat can be a real tonic in those situations. The session also helps you – through listening to the counsellor and the other members of the group – think about your relationship with food, and why it is that you fall back into the same unhealthy eating patterns time and time again. And yes, some nights I'd end up thinking that it might be just a load of mumbo-jumbo. Some nights I even thought, Do you know what? I could really do without this for an hour right now. But mostly these support sessions made me think about what got me to where I was now, and it was a fascinating process.

For instance, I'd never thought of myself as some-one who ate because I was unhappy. I'd never sat in the car jamming Hobnobs into my gob in secret like some of the people I heard speak. In fact I hadn't thought of my fatness as an issue at all. I didn't think I was a scoffer, no sir! I just enjoyed food. So what got me to 19-plus stone then? For me it was just too much food, too often over thirty years; and for me there always seemed to be a reason to eat.

Sitting back and watching other people eat had made me realize something else: people who are thin seem to manage food – and therefore their weight – without even thinking about it. They're weight managers. They know about portion control. My idea of portion control was covering the entire plate with food and making it slightly heaped – that's what I liked to see, a little sort of pyramid thing going on. From my observation it seemed that a non-fat person didn't suffer from the kind of 'portion dysmorphia' that I and a lot of other fat people do. They know that a portion of protein is about a handful, for example, and they know that they don't have to eat every single thing on their plate just because it's there. They seem to know it without even thinking about it. It's funny, because over the years I can remember people serving me massive plates of food and saying, 'If it's too much, just eat half of it, Pauline.' What they never under-stood was that it was impossible for me to 'just eat half of it'. It wasn't in my nature not to clear my plate.

When we were kids we were always told to eat up because there were children starving in Africa, but in the end, me eating far too much food all the time wasn't helping them, and it certainly wasn't helping me. I only had to glance around me when I was in a restaurant to see how differently I ate from a person who maintained a slimmer figure. Whereas I'd always have a starter – calamari or pâté, for instance – a weight manager might not have one at all. When I'd finished every bit of my main course, potato side dish and salad swimming in dressing an' all, the weight managers would have left what they didn't want. While I'd be tucking into the cheeseboard whether I was still hungry or not, those other strange and wonderful creatures might just share a dessert with their partner, and then only if they were still hungry.

All these things were becoming apparent to me as a spectator. But I knew that if I achieved my goal and got down to 11 stone on LighterLife, I was going to need to learn these seemingly alien skills for myself in order to keep the weight off.

For the first few weeks of being on the plan, my poor broken arm was still in its pot, so making food that only involved ripping a packet open with my teeth and pouring hot water over it seemed rather a godsend. I still had to exist in the real world, however, so I decided that although I wasn't eating regular food myself I wasn't going to forsake my love of it or turn away from one of my favourite pastimes – cooking! Mad, you might think, but no. Cooking helped give me a sense of perspective about food. After all, the world was still eating even if I wasn't, so I carried on watching my favourite cooking programmes on TV and I still made dinner for Steve and the kids whenever I was back at home. Further down the line, when Charley Webb from *Emmerdale* had a birthday party, I even did all the catering. It was my birthday present to her and I really enjoyed making my curry for all the guests. Of course, I couldn't taste the food, so I had Emily there to make sure the rice was cooked properly and the curry was just as it should be. When I was out at a restaurant with the family I'd still be enthusi-astically scrutinizing the menu and telling them all what I liked the look of.

'Ooh, that looks lovely, Charlie, are you gonna have that?' I'd say to my son, but I was always aware that I could only be a spectator. I couldn't play! Not for the moment. But that was OK.

5

The Body in the Bath

Meanwhile, while I was feeling a great deal more positive than I had before Christmas, my character on *Emmerdale*, Hazel Rhodes, was watching her life veer from bad to worse. When I first met with the producer Gavin Blyth, his idea had been for me to play a character called Joy, who had previously been in prison with Viv Hope.

I liked the sound of the part and I liked Gavin, so I said yes almost immediately, but I'd imagined it would be a short stint, so I suggested coming on board for three months. Gavin looked surprised, to say the least.

'The thing is, Pauline,' he said, 'we need time to introduce the character and build storylines around her and it usually takes a bit longer than three months to really establish a character.'

So by the time I'd left the office we were going with six months; then, after another phone call the next day, my agent said they were very excited about the prospect of having me and it had gone up to ten months! Of course the whole idea of the character changed quite a lot as time went on, and Joy became Hazel, but I really didn't expect to be playing her for so long. It was the longest stint I've ever done on anything in one go – eighteen months as it turned out.

In my biggest storyline, my on-screen son, Jackson, played by Marc Silcock, is critically injured when a train hits his car, and he ends up being paralysed from the shoulders down. Over the following months, as Hazel and Jackson's boyfriend, Aaron, try to help him come to terms with his awful disability, it becomes more and more apparent that Jackson can't stand the idea of living out his days as a tetraplegic and therefore wants to end his life. Eventually, he asks Hazel and Aaron to help him commit suicide. No, it's not very cheery, is it? However, for an actor it's a fantastic storyline to play and the two boys I was working closely with, Marc Silcock and Danny Miller, are such wonderful actors. There were some incredibly moving scenes between the three of us, and some days I came home from the set completely and utterly exhausted. (This was handy in the first few weeks of my LighterLife diet as I often ended up going to bed early and therefore had much less time to think about food!)

The thing I've found about playing a character who is in almost constant distress is that you have to force yourself, physically and mentally, to jump through hoops that you'd really rather not jump through: you're hunched over, you're sobbing, shouting, and getting yourself into a right old state. It really takes it out of you and sometimes my whole body hurt after a day's filming.

Despite a few headaches from crying so much and the physical exhaustion of it, though, I'm always aware that it is, at the end of the day, just pretend. Once the director yelled 'Cut' and I was off that set or out of that studio, I'd be wondering whether I'd get home in time to watch *Come Dine with Me*, or whichever of my favourite shows was on that particular evening. All I was thinking about was getting back to my flat and having a cuppa. I've never been an actress who takes the role home with her at night. In fact, the days when Danny, Marc and I had the heaviest and most emotionally overwrought acting to do on *Emmerdale* were generally the days we laughed the most – and quite often we really needed it!

One part of the story involved Hazel and Aaron taking Jackson on holiday to try to show him that life could still be worth living. Now we were all very excited about this trip, particularly when word had it that we were going to Barcelona. A few days later, however, the destination shifted, quite considerably: to Blackpool. Well, I for one was still quite excited as I'd never been to Blackpool, but I'm not sure the two lads were as keen on the idea as I was. Then we heard it was London, which the boys were keener on but not me, as I've lived there. Finally, it was announced that we were going to film the holiday scenes in Whitby. From Barcelona to Whitby! That's TV budgets in a recession, I guess. Still, I was very happy about going to Whitby and, despite the boys' obvious disappointment, it turned out to be a really good week.

Hazel and Aaron organize a skydive for Jackson while in Whitby, and Marc decided that he was going to jump out of the plane for real. On the day of filming, poor Marc was more than a tad nervous. The weather had been too bad the day before, when the jump had originally been scheduled, so he'd had a whole twenty-four hours to think about it.

The idea was that the second Marc landed he had to say a big piece of dialogue to camera, all in one shot.

'We'll have to get this right,' he said, anxiously. 'I'll do it once, but don't ask me to go up and do it again.'

When Marc safely hit the ground he remembered all his dialogue word for flamin' word and the shot was in the can. Perfect! The next shot, however, which was supposed to be a simple cutaway of Aaron and Hazel breathlessly watching Jackson as he descends, didn't go quite as smoothly. As the cameras rolled and Danny and I gazed up into the blue yonder, pretending to watch Jackson's spectacular feat of bravery in the face of terrible adversity, I pointed upwards and said, 'Look! He's waving, he's waving!'

'Cut!'

Everybody turned to look at me.

'Waving?' Marc smiled. 'I don't think so.'

I couldn't help it! I just got caught up in the excitement of it all, didn't I? Of course, the poor boy is supposed to be tetraplegic: i.e., paralysed from the neck down. That would make waving rather difficult, wouldn't it, Pauline? As I said,

I think I just got caught up in the excitement.

While we were in Whitby I was due to have one of my weekly LighterLife support group sessions. I was on location, so that week I was to do it as a conference call from my hotel room, back in Scarborough, at the usual time of eight o'clock. I decided to do it once I'd had a hot bath so I'd be nice and relaxed. We'd been outside filming all day and I was frozen to the bone, so climbing into a gorgeous, steamy bath was pretty much all I could think about. By the time I'd got back to the hotel and run the bath, though, it was very nearly eight o'clock, so I thought, sod it, I'll just take the phone with me and do the call while I'm soaking.

'I can hear water running, are you in the bath?' Mandy, my counsellor, asked me during our chat.

'I am,' I said. 'I've been freezing cold all day and it's lovely!'

Once I'd finished the call the water was getting a bit tepid so I decided it was time to get out. Uh-oh. Slight problem. I couldn't lift myself out of the bloody bath. I tried again as hard as I could, but to no avail. My arm was still weak and not completely healed from the break, and me being the size I am ... well, it just wasn't a good combination. I was well and truly stuck. My arms weren't strong enough to lift my body up and there was no handle on the bath to grab on to on the side of my stronger arm. Now what? I thought for a moment, trying to remain calm.

'Don't panic, don't panic,' I told myself. 'If I phone down to reception, reception can phone the *Emmerdale* make-up girls and they can come up to the room and help me. Great! Only they're not staying here tonight, are they? They're both staying with family tonight. Damn!'

Twenty minutes later, which might not sound a long time but certainly feels it when you're stuck in a cold bath not knowing how you're going to get out, I decided to have one more try at getting out on my own. I knew that whatever happened, I had to get myself out somehow. Perhaps it was the absolute dread of having to call someone from reception – male or female – to help me out of the bath that gave me the determination and strength to finally haul myself up and out; but it was agony and I was left shaking like a leaf at the end of it. It was a horrible experience.

I have to say that I did have more than a sideways glance at the room service menu that night. The old me might have said, 'Oh poor, poor Pauline! You've had such a terrible ordeal, you simply must have a cheesecake.' That's what I've done all my life, after all, not only when things have gone bad but also when they're good! But for the new me, not being able to do something as simple as getting out of a bath was all the more reason to keep on doing what I was doing. Perhaps I *was* now starting to change my behaviour and the way I thought about food.

6

The Sweet Sound of Angels

I'd become a great smeller of food! Yes, yes, I knew I couldn't eat it, but boy could I smell it. Ordinary coffee shops and sandwich bars suddenly turned into magnificent shrines rising up out of the pavement, with their tantalizing pastries and overstuffed breads laid out in front of me on the counter as if it were some kind of sacred altar. Untouchable. Forbidden. And so I sniffed . . . hard and long and as often as I could. I imagined how far my obsession with smelling real food might take me. Where will it all end, Pauline? I pictured myself loitering outside Greggs the bakers for hours, sniffing the air and eventually, unashamedly, licking the window, knowing I couldn't touch or eat the delicious baked goods within. I'd eventually be there for so long that the police would be summoned by the shop's staff to haul me, screaming and kicking, away from the window, and all the while I'd be begging them to let me loiter and worship for just a few moments more, outside that sacred temple of flaky pastry. The next day's paper would carry the sombre headline: *Emmerdale star arrested in sausage roll sniffing debacle*. I could see it all so clearly.

On 18 February 2011, six weeks after I started on the programme, I had my first big test with real food. Danny Miller had brilliantly, and single-handedly, organized a huge charity ball at the Marriott in Manchester to raise money for Macmillan Cancer Support. This big charity fundraiser was in memory of Gavin Blyth, who had died suddenly and unexpectedly of lymphoma in November 2010. The event included a sit-down three-course dinner with alcohol on the table, a proper showbiz event (and we can knock it back when we want to, as I'm sure you know) and a dietary disaster waiting to happen as far as I was concerned. Should I even be going and putting temptation in my way? It would have been much easier to just stay home; but I really wanted to go in memory of Gavin, who had offered me the job on

Emmerdale in the first place, and out of respect to Danny, who I'm very fond of. So I did.

My daughter Emily came with me and we booked ourselves into the Marriott, making sure I took my packs with me. I ate one before we went downstairs to the do, so at least I knew I wouldn't be starving hungry, and as it turned out, getting through the meal was a lot easier than I'd imagined. Although the people on my table didn't know I was on any kind of eating plan, when the first course came along they were far too busy tucking into their own grub to notice that I had pushed mine to the side. When the chicken and mashed potato main course came, I played about with it a bit, cut the chicken in half and gave some to Emily and didn't eat a thing. Still, because my food looked as though it had been touched, nobody was any the wiser. When the wine came round time and time again I just stuck with fizzy water. The funny thing was that it didn't even feel like I was denying myself anything. I still had a really good time and enjoyed everyone's company – we had a great laugh! The only reason I finally went upstairs at around midnight was because everyone else was rather drunk, which, as I'm sure you know, can get a bit boring when you're the only one who's stone cold sober. The bottom line was that I'd gone to a big, boozy, food-filled social event, had a really good time, not fallen off the wagon diet-wise, and no one was any the wiser.

Sitting up in my hotel room that night opening my snack bar, I remember saying to myself, 'Do you know what, Pauline? I think you might have cracked this. I really think you might have cracked it!'

It was pretty much the same story when we went out for Emily's birthday a couple of weeks later: I still enjoyed myself, I just focused on the conversation and the company rather than the food and wine. What was the alternative? Locking myself away in a broom cupboard until the weight had fallen off. In the past I'd have said, 'Oh, I'll skip the diet tonight, it's so-and-so's birthday, or I'm on holiday this week so I'll go back on the diet next week.' Sound familiar? Well, I suddenly realized that it was always going to be someone's birthday. There was always going to be a holiday or a social event. There was always going to be cake! I just had to get on with my life, charity balls an' all, while I was losing this weight, or my social life was going to be non-existent.

The thing is I'd never believed that I had willpower before, and over the years, with all my failed attempts at diets, particularly the one I started in the summer of 2010, I think I used that lack of willpower as an excuse to fail without even realizing it. I was wrong. Sticking to my LighterLife diet, strict as it was, had been a massive achievement for me, and boy was I sticking to it. After a difficult first few weeks, when it was really hard to actually see the weight coming off (and let's face it, folks, that was because there was a lot of it to come off), I was finally beginning to see some results. That really made a difference, I can tell you. It's not like I noticed day by day that I was getting thinner or that my clothes were too big, but something was happening, albeit gradually, and I suddenly felt positive that I'd made the right decision at the start of the year.

Remember, I was a woman who could quite happily scoff a cheese roll while waiting for my dinner to cook, but now I was sticking to my packs and that was that. I could remember what cheese tasted like, and though I loved that taste I certainly didn't love it as much as the changes I was now seeing in my body shape. Besides, I'd be able to eat cheese again one day in the not too distant future, right? So for now I'd just stick with the memory of it. Of course, I had the commitment to LighterLife to consider as well. I knew that once it was all out in the open that I was being sponsored by them to lose weight on their plan, certain people would be just itching to catch a glimpse of me outside McDonald's with a quarter pounder in my gob – that's just human nature, I guess. So I didn't want to let LighterLife down, no.

That wasn't the main reason I was so resolute, though. First and foremost it was about me! I was doing this for me now. I'd made a commitment to myself and I was going to stick to it. It was my last chance. And when all that weight had come off, all that eight and a half stone I was determined to get rid of, I had to be able to look back and say, 'I did that for me!'

After the first couple of months on the pro-gramme I'd lost about 2 stone 9lb in weight and after another month I'd lost 3 stone 10. If that wasn't an incentive to keep going, I didn't know what was. I kept happily remembering the first time that somebody outside the family commented on how good I was starting to look: it was lovely Zoe Henry, who plays vet Rhona Goskirk on *Emmerdale*. We were sitting in the Woolpack pub and she suddenly said to me, 'You look well.'

'Thanks,' I smiled in return.

'You've lost weight, haven't you?' she went on.

'Yes, I have.'

I thought for a moment I could hear angels singing. It was just wonderful. Well, as the weeks went by there would be another remark about how good I was looking, and then another. I wondered how long it would be before the writers of *Emmerdale* would have to mention Hazel's weight loss in the script because it was so noticeable. Wow! Would that actually happen? The thought of it became a wonderful scenario I'd play in my head over and over. It was another thing to spur me on.

At that time, my *Emmerdale* alter ego, Hazel, was getting herself in a right old state and the emotionally draining scenes were coming thick and fast. If there was one scene that completely took it out of me, both physically and mentally, it was the one where Hazel finally agrees to help Jackson end his life by assisted suicide. This was a huge emotional scene for both Marc and myself, and while we were really pleased with the results we agreed that we wouldn't want to put ourselves through it again. The two of us were full-on sobbing during the takes and I, for one, was totally shattered afterwards.

The whole *Emmerdale* set had recently moved to new studios and we were suddenly made aware that there was a problem with the water pipes in certain parts of the new building, or at least the sound of them. The sound department were picking up the flushing of cisterns every time somebody went to the loo, rendering certain scenes unusable. And yep, you guessed it! My Oscar-deserving performance with Marc was one of them and we were told that we'd have to do the scene all over again.

'No, please don't tell me I have to do that again, not that one,' I pleaded.

Unfortunately, there was no way round it. Not only did we have to reshoot the scene, but because of the pipes the crew also had to move the whole set of Hazel's house back to the old studio, which was now like a ghost town. Can you imagine? You do one of the most gut-wrenching scenes of your entire career, give it your absolute all, and then someone goes and ruins it by flushing the khazi!

As my momentous storyline continued, the weeks went on and the weight came off, and eventually I started to feel really good. I stuck rigidly to my plan as if it was the most important mission on earth, and I guess to me at that time it was. There were some weeks when my weigh-in was rather less inspiring than others. In fact, one week in May I somehow managed to actually put on a pound, but that's how it goes. Still, I was undeterred, and the encouragement and support I was getting from the people around me at *Emmerdale* completely bowled me over, especially once I'd finally gone public about doing Lighter-Life. I never once had someone come up to me and say, 'Oh what are you doing that rubbish for? Have a bit of cake, it won't hurt just this once.'

Have you noticed how some people do that? Sometimes if you've always been the fat girl in a group of thin girls, the others don't really want you to lose weight, do they? That's your thing. She's the smart one, she's the pretty one, she's the flirty one . . . and you're the fat one! So people say things like 'Don't lose any more, you've lost enough now. You won't look like you any more.' And there you are, still 16 stone! Well, there was none of that from the wonderful girls at *Emmerdale*.

'Pauline, you look fantastic!'

'Pauline, we're so proud of you.'

The girls even offered to eat their food out of sight before coming to sit with me to keep temptation out of my way, but I didn't need or want that, to be honest.

'Don't be daft, come and sit down with me,' I'd tell them.

The fantastic words of encouragement I was getting from these girls was better than any cheese and pickle roll, I can tell you: these gorgeous actresses, all slim and svelte, and not a bitchy or discouraging word amongst them. Lucy Pargeter, who had become my Mrs Fix-it, even suggested a gym for me to join when I mentioned that I fancied having a go at some exercise. Yes, you heard right! I'd decided I was ready to join a gym. The world's gone mad!

One day I got a script where Hazel's weight loss was finally mentioned. Of course, she's going through a really bad time after making the decision to help Jackson commit suicide, and we did a scene in the café where Bob, played by Tony Audenshaw, offers Hazel some cake, saying that she looks like she needs feeding up. Hazel then says something along the lines of 'That's what stress does to you, Bob.' Finally! My weight loss had by now become so obvious that the scriptwriters had had to write it in. That fabulous scenario that I'd played over and over in my head had actually come true.

'I've dreamed about this,' I told Tony afterwards with a grin.

'You deserve it,' he replied. 'You deserve every bit of it.'

It may not sound like a big thing to everyone, but to me it was a fantastic milestone and I was over the moon. For the first time in thirty years, Pauline Quirke was getting thinner.

7

The Trappings of Fame

I did occasionally wonder, as I seemed to be literally shrinking before people's eyes on a primetime soap opera, what the public's reaction might be to my weight loss. I mean, if I really did hit my target after months of dieting, would their perception of me change? It was actually quite timely for Hazel to be losing weight, going through terrible grief, but what about Pauline Quirke? Like it or not, I was a famous face and on television five nights a week, so shedding eight and a half stone was hardly something I could do under the radar. I guess it was just one of the accessories that go along with being in the public eye and so there was no point worrying about it, was there?

As far as being an actress was concerned I'd never felt overly self-conscious about my weight. You see, I quite like me and I always have and I have never had any illusions that being thinner would make me a better or happier person, or, indeed, solve all of life's problems in one fell swoop. The truth is, I've always thought I was a pretty OK person even though I was carrying around a few extra pounds . . . all right, a few extra stone! Similarly, I've never accepted an acting role that called for someone to be fat and not much else; 'fat-girl' parts, if you will. The characters I played happened to be overweight simply because I was, but their fatness was not the sum of them. Sure, in *Birds of a Feather* there were plenty of cracks about Sharon being overweight – usually from Dorien – but there were also comments about Tracey being a bit dim or Dorien being promiscuous. Sharon was much more than just plump and the other characters I've chosen to play over the years have never been defined by their weight.

That's not to say there haven't been a few sticky casting moments. I recall with some embarrassment, for instance, the time I was asked to do a television drama called *Murder in Mind*, and at the first meeting with the producer he told me what a big fan of mine he was, which is always nice. I was really looking forward to doing this show, particularly as I got to chuck somebody off the top of a tower block, something which, bizarrely, appealed to me no end – in an acting role sort-of-a-way only, of course. Anyway, going back to this first meeting once I'd got the part, I sat down in a room with the producer and the director, and the producer carried on enthusing about my past work.

'I have to say, now I've got the opportunity, that I loved that drama you were in a while back, Pauline. Where you played a nurse who killed her patients. You were absolutely fabulous in that.'

Well, I was slightly confused for a minute, until it dawned on me that the play he'd been referring to was, in fact, *Tender Loving Care* . . . starring Dawn French!

I sat there while he waxed lyrical about my marvellous performance in a drama that I wasn't even in, not quite knowing what to do. I mean, does one say, 'I'm sorry, that wasn't me, love, it was Dawn French'? Surely that would just embarrass him, and God knows I was embarrassed enough for the both of us. So I decided to keep my mouth shut. In fact, not only did I keep my mouth shut, I also nodded and smiled, actually taking credit for all the

Above: With my mum, Hetty. You could say I got my love of food and cooking from her – she was such a good cook.

Below: I'm guessing I took this picture with my Polaroid as I'm the only one not in it! *Left to right*: Mum, my niece Kerrie, my sister Kitty and my brother Sean.

Above: Some beautifully staged publicity shots taken after joining Anna Scher's drama club. I mean, who leaves their slippers by the fire like that?

Below: These are actually both from the 1974 BBC *Play for Today* called 'Eleanor'. I'd helpfully mucked up the continuity by going and getting my hair cut.

Above: Aged eighteen or so on the set of the LWT series *Lovely Couple* with Elaine Donnelly and Anthony O'Donnell. Up to the age of sixteen you were accompanied by a chaperone on any job. After that you were given your train timetable and expected to find your own way there!

Below: As Veronica 'with the eye' in *Shine on Harvey Moon*, with Linda Robson and Lee Whitlock. Pregnant with my daughter Emily at the time, the strategically positioned sofa does a remarkable job of hiding the baby bump.

Above: A still from the original *Birds of a Feather* title sequence in which Linda and I walked around under spotlights. It looked a bit too serious for a sit-com, apparently, and was scrapped after the first series.

Below: With Lesley and Linda in one of the many *Birds of a Feather* Christmas specials we did – this one in Majorca. Linda was pregnant this time around with her son Louis.

In the end *Birds of a Feather* ran for 102 episodes over nine years. *Clockwise from top*: as would-be entrepreneurs with our new cleaning business 'Maids of Ongar'; holding a séance when Tracey's convinced the house is haunted; and off to LA to track down George Hamilton, convinced he's Sharon and Tracey's father. Oh, and bumping into Richard Branson on the way, as you do.

Above: The water cart's off again after a genuine surprise on *This Morning*. I hadn't heard from Linda for ages and was so worried about her. To think she'd just been too scared to talk to me in case she spoiled it all!

Below: With Linda and Lesley on *The Alan Titchmarsh Show* in October 2011 to talk about the upcoming *Birds of a Feather* stage tour.

Right: With my great friend Linda again, performing live on *Children in Need* as ABBA. Hand on heart, it was one of the most nerve-racking things I've ever had to do.

Below: Another sketch for *Children in Need*, this time written by yours truly. Fed up with getting stuck with all the frumpy outfits, it was time for a swap in the glamour stakes. And yes, Bacofoil dresses were the height of glamour at the time.

All hot and sweaty on location in the Grand Canyon for a holiday programme. The shot was meant to be used for publicity purposes, but apparently it didn't look real enough and we ended up reshooting it in a studio when we got back!

stellar work that Dawn had done in the drama and basking in her glory. OK, so maybe all us fat girls look the same, I thought.

Apart from that, my weight hasn't been too much of an issue over the years, TV-wise, unless you count the time I was on *Celebrity Who Wants to Be a Millionaire* with Max Clifford. We were there to raise money for the Rhys Daniels Trust, of which Max and I are both patrons. Don't get me wrong, I wasn't so much worried about not being able to answer any difficult questions, but I *was* petrified about whether or not I would be able to get up on the bloody stool! Well, it was about ten feet off the ground (or at least it seemed like it was to me) and I knew in rehearsals that I wasn't going to make it, so I said to Chris Tarrant, 'Chris, you're going to have to help me up, I'm a fat cow and I can't get up on the stool.'

Of course, Chris helped me up on the night in front of the entire audience, and I was a little embarrassed but at least I made it. The stool was stupidly high, I tell you! Anyway, to add insult to injury, someone had felt the need to put a cushion on it for me. Great! It wasn't quite as bad as the seatbelt saga, but there were definitely more than a few blushes from me that evening.

Where Have I Gone?

I usually tend to shy away from shows with the word 'celebrity' in the title, to be honest. I did do *Celebrity Masterchef* because I love cooking and I was incredibly excited about the prospect of cooking in a professional kitchen, but unfortunately I didn't make it past the first round so that was that. Then recently my whole family were on *All Star Family Fortunes*, which was great fun.

Now I've been watching *Family Fortunes* for 30-odd years and I can talk you through every presenter: Max Bygraves, Bob Monkhouse, Les Dennis and now Vernon Kay – I'm a big fan! But watching a quiz show from the comfort of your living-room sofa, where you can answer all the questions perfectly, is a completely different kettle of fish from actually being there in front of an audience, not to mention the cameras. Bearing in mind that my husband and son are extremely competitive and hate to lose – they just can't help themselves – I said to Steve, Emily, Lauren (my stepdaughter) and Charlie beforehand, 'Let's not make a big thing of it or get stressed out, let's just enjoy it.'

In rehearsals everything went fine and dandy. Emily and I practised the 'head-to-head' section and did brilliantly, mainly thanks to Emily getting 198 points out of a possible 200, leaving me only two points to get. During the recording of the show, however, things didn't work out quite so well. We were playing against Jo Whiley's family, who were really lovely, but some of our answers in the heat of the moment, I feel, were not the same ones we would have yelled at the TV screen from the comfort of our own sofa with a cup of tea and a packet of biscuits. Charlie, my sixteen-year-old son, for example, spends half his life with his eyes glued to a smartphone or an iPad or a computer of some sort, like most teenagers, I suppose. So it was no surprise when he hit the buzzer first to guess what the top answer in a survey of 100 people might be to the question: How would you send a message? Now bear in mind that this is a boy who would normally have to have his mobile phone surgically removed from his hand on most days. Nevertheless his answer to the question was . . . post it! What? WHAT? Post it? Of course the top answer was text, but it's amazing how the intellect you seem to have in your living room deserts you in the heat of the moment under those studio lights. Needless to say, we came second. True, other people might call that losing, but I prefer to say we came second.

So that's about the sum of me being a so-called celebrity, which is fine by me as I'm not a big fan of that word to begin with. I much prefer to think of myself as someone who is privileged enough to have a really fantastic job. Fame and what people call celebrity have only landed at my door because I've been successful in the work I've done over the past forty years as an actress. That's why I went into the business, because I wanted to perform and act. People who go into the entertainment business just because they want to be famous are doing it the wrong way round as far as I'm concerned. Yes, fame is a by-product of my success as an actress but to me it's still a job. When I'm getting changed to go home after a day's filming I'm invariably thinking about whether I'll catch the shops still open on the way home, or whether I need a bottle of bleach or not because I've spotted a buy-one-get-one-free offer on in Sainsbury's at the weekend. When I stop work, I stop.

Believe it or not, one of the upsides of my job on *Emmerdale* was getting up at stupid o'clock to stand in the middle of a field (or some other outdoor location) in the peeing rain and then getting paid for it. Yes, that was an upside! I still love what I do and being on *Emmerdale* completely reaffirmed that fact for me. I think I'd fallen out of love with my acting career a little bit before I started on *Emmerdale*, to be honest. For the previous couple of years before starting on the show I had gone from job to job with hardly a break in between. Now don't get me wrong, for an actor that's a pretty fabulous position to be in, but I felt like I was missing out on a lot of stuff when it came to my home life and my family. Goodness knows, Charlie still remembers the one parents' evening I never made it to (he's forgotten the twenty-two I did get to, but that's kids for you). But I felt like I was working so hard that I was missing out on all the things I was supposedly working hard for. So, as I was lucky enough to be in a position where I could take some time out, that's what I did. I took eighteen months off and basically did mini-cabbing for my children for the duration of it.

'Quirke's cabs, at your service!'

I did need that time away, though, as I've been working pretty much non-stop since I was nine years old, and that brief stint as an ordinary wife, mother and mini-cab driver made me appreciate how lucky I am to have both: a happy family life and a great job. Being on *Emmerdale* reminded me how much I love my work, too. It reminded me how much I love the company of other actors, how much I love to watch good actors working – and God knows there are plenty of those on *Emmerdale*. It was definitely one of the best experiences of my working life, even though I've sometimes been away from my family for long periods.

As far as the downsides of being famous go, I'm hard pushed to think of many, to tell you the truth. Yes, there are times when being recognized and people asking for your autograph or photograph might be a slight inconvenience, but it's hardly the end of your world, is it? Quite honestly, if you're sitting in Wimpy (do they still exist?) having a quiet burger you're probably not going to be bothered. If, however, you've had one over the eight and you're inconspicuously falling out of The Ivy at eleven o'clock at night, chances are you'll be spotted and get your picture taken. If you go to a film premiere, you'll undoubtedly have autographs to sign and pictures to pose for on the red carpet, but then again if you don't like it you should have taken yourself down Holloway Road Odeon to watch the bloody film, and then nobody would have been any the wiser. It's your choice most of the time, although there have been a few occasions when being recognized has caught me somewhat unawares. It can be quite embarrassing.

A few years back I was standing up on a packed 73 bus in Oxford Street, when an old girl sitting nearby, who was clearly a bit hard of hearing, started bellowing at me across the aisle.

''Ere! I know you, dun' I? I know you!'

So I smiled and nodded politely, not wanting to draw attention to myself.

'Yeah, yeah,' she went on. 'You're em . . . you're . . .'

'I'm on the telly,' I said as discreetly as you can on a packed bus in Oxford Street. 'You might have seen me on the telly.'

But she wasn't having it, and she was loud. Boy she was loud!

'No, no, that ain't it, love, no. I've seen you . . .'

'I'm an actress,' I assured her, now feeling a bit uncomfortable. 'You've probably seen me on the telly, dear.'

'No,' she said, 'you work down the hearing aid centre in Stepney, don't ya? That's it.'

'No! I don't, I'm an actress, I . . .'

'Yes, yes, I seen you down at the hearing aid centre. That's why I know ya – from down the hearing aid centre.'

So I just gave up and nodded.

More recently, in 2009 I was doing a charity book signing at WH Smith in Beaconsfield, in aid of the Iain Rennie Hospice charity, of which I'm a big supporter. Every year the charity publishes a book called *Rhyme and Reason*, which is a collection of poems by local people, and we do a special book signing at the local WH Smith. It's always Fern Britton, the actor Geoffrey Palmer or me doing the honours and we'd take it in turns. Now the branch of Smith's in Beaconsfield isn't that roomy to start with, and the space we were allocated seemed to be shrinking by the year. This particular year they decided that the only place they could stick me was in front of the drinks cabinet, which is a very small space indeed.

So there I am trying to look important enough to sign books for anyone who might want one, while people are coming up to my table to ask me if I can kindly open the fridge door and get them a drink out! And while I'm at it could I possibly lean across and pass them up a copy of *Horse and Hound* as well? I'm literally sitting there signing books one minute, then standing up to open the fridge and pass a can of Coke to some kid who then says, 'Nah, actually can I have a Lilt?'

So I open the fridge door again, put the Coke back, and get the kid a Lilt.

During the course of the day a fellow came up to the table and took an interest in the book.

'Why are you signing?' he asked me.

'It's a book of poems for the Iain Rennie Hospice charity,' I cheerily replied.

'Oh,' he said, 'and who are you?'

'My name's Pauline Quirke, I'm an actress,' I said, still smiling amiably.

'Oh yes,' he nodded, vaguely. 'I don't like you.'

'Fair enough,' I said, slightly taken aback. 'Well, would you like a book anyway?'

'Not really,' he said, and then he was gone.

At least he was honest, I suppose.

What really fascinates me is when people see you on the TV all the time, they think they actually *do* know you, and can therefore say or do whatever they damn well please. As I said, most of the time it's lovely, but some situations can be a bit odd or just downright farcical. Once, when Linda Robson and me were doing a holiday programme for the BBC at the Grand Canyon, we suddenly heard these booming northern accents echoing across the abyss.

'SHARON! TRACEY! SHARON! TRACEY!'

Some *Birds of a Feather* fans had spotted us a mile off and were yelling our screen characters' names out at the tops of their voices. It just sounded so bizarre bouncing around the vastness of the Grand

Canyon in the middle of the Arizona desert; we couldn't stop laughing.

I've even had people recognize me on holiday, around the pool. They'll edge their sunbeds nearer and nearer until they're close enough for a cosy chat.

'Can we have a picture with you please?' they'll say.

'Of course!' I'll reply obligingly, and the next day they might do the same and probably the next.

By the end of the week, although the novelty of having a 'celeb' in their midst has completely worn off for them, the sense of familiarity certainly hasn't. The same woman will tap me on the shoulder while I'm sunbathing or reading.

'Can you take a picture of me with my aunt Sadie, please, Pauline?'

'Oh, you don't want me in it?'

'No, can you just take it?'

'I am on holiday, you know.'

'Oh, go on, just the one!'

Another rather peculiar situation is to bump into a fan when you're being treated in hospital. A male nurse was attending to me once – well, when I say 'attending' what I actually mean is that he was 'preparing' me for my Caesarean section. Yes, you know what I mean, girls, razor in hand an' all.

'Ooh! I'm a huge fan of *Birds of a Feather*,' he trilled as he skilfully shaved away. 'I love it, I do!'

Then he proceeded to rattle on about how much he enjoyed the show as he went merrily about his business while I just lay there looking up at him, not knowing quite what to say. That was a weird one. I was even asked for an autograph when I was tending my mother's grave once, which was definitely a step too far, and my sister gave the perpetrators very short shrift, I can tell you.

But as I said before I can't really complain. You get a million and one people who are absolutely lovely, but there's always one who just doesn't pick the right moment. Still, I try to remember that it's the public who pay my wages and keep me employed, so I've learned to accept the good – and the not so good – trappings of fame.

8

A Red Carpet Moment

I'm not going to pretend that everything was rosy all the time while I was on this strict diet. It certainly wasn't! There were a couple of moments during the long months of abstinence when I seriously wondered whether it was all worth it, particularly on the slow weeks when my weight loss barely registered on the scales. One particular week, I felt very low when I got on to the scales and discovered that I'd lost hardly any weight at all.

'I've lost one pound eight ounces this week,' I moaned at Steve and Emily. 'One pound eight ounces! I could have lost that with a bloody good sneeze.'

I felt like I'd been working at it long and hard, and I was very despondent.

'I've been so good, this is *not* fair,' I said. 'I'm really, really peed off!'

Luckily I wasn't peed off enough to go and grab the nearest cheese sandwich straight away, but I certainly needed talking down. I suddenly found myself at a point when it would have been very easy for me to throw in the towel because I felt so down.

'Mum, just put that one pound eight ounces together with what you've already lost,' Emily told me. 'Think about the total. You've done so well.'

I knew she was right, but it was hard. Still, after a long chat with her and Steve, both of them fantastic as always, I took myself upstairs for a nice hot bath, and then I went to bed early with a good magazine. Tomorrow was another day. Disaster averted!

The counsellor said much the same to me at the weekly meeting.

'It's never going to be the same huge weight loss it was the first week. You're never going to shed another ten or eleven pounds in a week again. Just look at how much you have lost in all and then add this amount on to the total. Focus on what you're going to achieve next week.'

So that's what I did, and I got through it. The following week I lost about 4lb and I was happy with that. And as long as the weight kept going down I would try to stay happy. After all, I'd never considered myself a yo-yo dieter before doing LighterLife: my weight had just gone up . . . and up . . . and up!

On the night of the British Soap Awards in May, four and a half months after I'd started the diet, I was down to 14 stone 2. I'd lost almost six stone and the change in my body shape was, as you can probably imagine, pretty drastic. I hadn't cheated or veered off the plan once, and the truth of the matter was that nothing I could eat was going to taste as good as the fantastic feedback I was getting from everyone around me. Apart from becoming the incredible shrinking woman, I was also noticing something quite interesting about my body that I'd almost forgotten: I actually had bones! Yes, folks, I was discovering them sticking out all over the place: my shoulders, my arms. In fact, when I was in the shower each morning it was like I was washing somebody else entirely. Yuk! Did you know you've got bones in your bum? Did you? Well I didn't, but there they were! In bed of a night I felt like a drawer of loose cutlery rattling around the mattress – it was *weird*. I felt like I couldn't get comfortable because there were all these funny bits sticking out of me all over the shop.

'What are these things here? Shoulder blades? Well I never.'

Despite having this bizarre biological phenomenon to become accustomed to, I was actually feeling good about what I'd achieved over the past few months. Just the fact that I was able to live without alcohol for five months was a revelation in itself. Who knew I didn't need wine? I certainly didn't up till that point. I'd downed a glass of wine or two every night for years. There were no food cravings either, which was a relief. What I was craving was being able to get on that aeroplane on my upcoming holiday without having to worry about needing an extension belt. I was craving the experience of sitting by the pool in a swimming costume without a cleverly placed towel or some sort of robe around me. The meat and potato pie could go take a running jump!

By now everyone knew I was on the LighterLife plan. I'd come out of the larder, so to speak, and at work I had nothing but support and encouragement from everyone. By this time I'd begun to eat my packs in the green room with everyone else, and nobody questioned it or even mentioned it. In fact the only references to my diet were to do with the positive effect it was clearly having on me, both physically and mentally. People were behind me. Even the folks in the costume department at *Emmerdale* were more than happy to keep finding me clothes in smaller sizes as the weight came off, although I hadn't done very much clothes shopping myself: I didn't see the point while my size was still changing all the time.

So, back to the Soap Awards in May. Now usually I'm not good with award ceremonies, I have to say, particularly all that marching up and down the red carpet malarkey and having your photograph taken from every unfavourable angle. I just never wanted to do it. Most of the time I couldn't find anything to wear and if I did stumble across a half-decent outfit I knew it wasn't going to look all that great anyway, me being the size that I was.

In 1997 I was nominated for a BAFTA for my role in *The Sculptress*, and that award ceremony was a torturous enough experience to last me a lifetime. Apart from having to decide what I was going to wear and worrying about how I would look on the red carpet, I also wanted to go for a wee from the very second I sat down in my nice prime seat at the Royal Albert Hall. Three and a half hours I sat there busting for the toilet. I was too scared to get up and go during the awards in case my category came up and I missed it. Imagine!

'And the award goes to Pauline Quirke for *The Sculptress*.'

'Can you 'ang on, mate, she's in the bog!'

So I just sat there with my legs crossed. Once they did announce the winner of the best actress category – and it wasn't me, anyway – I still didn't feel I could get up to go to the loo in case people thought I had the needle because I hadn't won and was storming off in a strop. So that was another hour. Nightmare!

Anyway, the 2011 Soap Awards in Manchester were an altogether different experience. The fact that I was able to glam myself up and look at clothes that I'd never had the chance to even consider before made a hell of a difference to the entire experience. I was nominated for 'best newcomer' (which is a bit strange when you've been in the business for forty years, but then again I *was* new to soap) and when I hit that red carpet it felt magical. I wore a gorgeous grey dress with black lace trim that I chose and bought myself in Monsoon, topped off with a little black bolero cardigan. I felt really great. I felt special. Why wouldn't I? I hadn't bought a dress for about thirty years.

Now usually at these dos I'm out of that car and down that red carpet so fast you don't see me for dust, but that night they almost had to get a shepherd's crook round my neck to haul me off the bloody thing. You've never seen anyone milk it so much as when I stepped out of that car and paraded in front of the crowd – it was like I was moving in slow motion. In fact, I had so many photographs taken that there was a backlog of *Coronation Street* cast members all waiting for me to move so that they could get on with their red carpet walks. Still, I was having my moment and they could wait. I felt terrific.

Once the awards got under way I just relaxed and enjoyed myself. I still get very star-struck when I see people from *Coronation Street* and other television shows I'm a fan of so I do have to keep myself under control to make sure I don't embarrass myself too much, but it was all very exciting nonetheless. Although I didn't win in my category, we were all so chuffed that Danny Miller won in his, which was best actor.

There were a few other priceless moments to be had as well. When Phillip Schofield announced that *EastEnders* had won best soap, which is the final award of the evening, Shane Richie, who plays Alfie in *EastEnders*, grabbed Mark Charnock, who plays Marlon in *Emmerdale*, and dragged him up on the stage along with the entire *EastEnders* cast. Mark has got to be one of the tallest actors on television, so at the end of this glamorous awards ceremony there he is, our Marlon, up there on stage towering above most of the *'Enders* cast, grinning for all to see. Well, at least we got someone up there for the Best Soap award!

The other brilliant moment was when Tony Prescott (one of *Emmerdale*'s lovely directors, who had previously worked on *Coronation Street*) got up to accept an award for his part in the fantastic fiftieth-anniversary live episode of *Corrie*, which included the spectacular tram crash and its dramatic aftermath. Poor Tony – surely in the heat of the moment – must have forgotten who some of his audience were, because after he'd wholeheartedly thanked all of the *Coronation Street* cast, he went on to declare enthusiastically that they were indeed 'the finest actors in the world'.

'What? What did he just say?'

You can just imagine the *Emmerdale* mob – the people he was currently working with every day – being horrified that their director had just announced that the cast of a rival soap were the best actors in the world. It was actually rather funny, and poor Tony has had so much stick about it ever since. He'll probably never live it down.

After the awards ceremony, Emily and I headed back to the hotel in Manchester where we'd glammed up earlier in the evening. We were only stopping to get our bits and pieces together before driving straight back to Leeds that night. I'd decided that as I wasn't drinking anyway I might as well do that rather than spend the next morning driving. So once we'd both changed out of our glamorous attire and back into our civvies, I went down to the front desk and handed in the receipt I'd been given earlier by the valet parking man, all ready to collect my car.

'I'm sorry, I don't know what you're talking about, madam, we don't provide valet parking,' the bloke on reception said.

'What?'

'We don't have valet parking.'

'But I gave my keys in! I've got a receipt!'

'We don't have valet parking, madam.'

I turned to Emily in confusion and went back over what had happened when we'd arrived at the hotel earlier that day. I'd walked into the lobby and up to the reception desk, where a man had been standing.

'Do you do valet parking?' I'd said.

'Yes,' he'd replied.

So I had promptly handed him the keys of my Range Rover. What was the problem?

Suddenly a veil of utter horror descended over me. Had I just handed some random bloke the keys to my beautiful car – simply because he was hovering around the reception desk of a hotel looking hospitable? Had I literally given my car away four hours earlier?

An hour went by of me sweating and trying to make this receptionist understand the seriousness of what was happening here. Suddenly there was a breakthrough! It transpired that they did have valet parking but it finished at 8 pm and he couldn't help me. By this time it was midnight. With panic still rising, I abandoned the unhelpful receptionist and located a woman who worked at the hotel and told her about my plight. She phoned the car park employees, who duly informed her that they did indeed have my car (phew!) and that they would bring it back to me. Panic over! Or so it seemed.

Fifteen minutes later, however, when the car hadn't turned up, I wearily made my way back to the reception desk to the original man I'd been getting nowhere with.

'Have you heard anything about my car yet?' I asked, hopefully. 'There's a man from the car park coming to drop it off to me, but he's certainly taking his time.'

'Oh yes,' he said. 'He's been and now he's gone again.'

'So where's my car then?'

'He didn't bring your car, or the keys,' the man said.

I felt like I was in a parallel universe. It was now almost an hour and a half since I'd first arrived at the desk and I just wanted to get back to Leeds. Was that too much to ask?

'Right,' I said to the man, as calmly as possible. 'I'm going to have to call the police, I'm afraid, because five hours ago I handed over the keys to my car and, as far as I can make out, you're refusing to give it back to me!'

He just didn't seem to get it, though. His attitude was: Oh forget about it! Forget about your lovely Range Rover, love, what's the matter with you? Chill out!

Eventually, after virtual hysteria, I got the car back, but by that time the glitz and glamour of the soap awards had all but melted away.

9

Rewards

I decided to reward myself for having done as well as I had on the diet. In times of old I'd have treated myself to a slap-up Indian takeaway or a nice bottle of wine. This time, though, I decided to reward myself with . . . a bike. Yes, believe it or not, that's what I wanted most of all: my first bike at the age of fifty-two. It wasn't just any old bike either: it was a fantastic bike. It was the dog's bollocks of bikes! I went all the way to Manchester to get it: didn't care if I could get it in the car or not, I was having it! It had flowers on it, it had a basket, and it had a bell. It was just lovely! I could be Mary Poppins on this bike, I thought, as I drove home with it. I could get a little terrier dog to put in the basket at the front. I was, as you can probably tell, very excited about this bike.

I also started going to the gym because I now felt like I could. It was another reward I gave myself (and let me tell you, I'd never have considered gym membership a reward before). I didn't go stark raving mad at first, no, but fifteen minutes on the treadmill here and there, plus a few little goes on some of the other apparatus that I'd have previously found utterly terrifying, and I was away. These were my treats, like walking down the red carpet at the soap awards was my personal reward. Of course, not everyone gets to do that, so you have to discover your own red carpet, I believe. We do need to like ourselves a bit more and reward ourselves too. God knows, I spent enough time beating myself up about being fat over the years, as do many overweight people. We need to know when it's time to pat ourselves on the back too.

I was looking forward to getting down to a size where I could wear a beautiful suede jacket that I'd had for a while. It had never looked good on me as, of course, it was too small. Anyway, I finally decided to give it a whirl and try it on, but what do you know, it was too big! It hung off me and looked ridiculous. I'd only missed the flamin' window when my lovely jacket would have actually fitted me. I also bought a rather snazzy pair of white jeans from Marks & Spencer that I couldn't wait to get into, but by the time I had a chance to wear them I'd lost another half a stone and they were too big and baggy: another window come and gone. I decided that it really was pointless buying new clothes until I'd almost reached my target. Fat people panic buy, you see, and so I had all sorts of stuff that I couldn't wear. Once, when I had an event coming up and nothing to wear, I rushed off to Harrods in desperation. Panic buying in Harrods – really sensible, Pauline! Still, at the time I thought that Harrods would surely have some 'nice fat-clothes'. As it turned out they didn't really, but I grabbed a turquoise dress anyway because I love the colour. I never did wear it, in fact it still had the label on when I picked it up at the start of June 2011 to try it on, but, again, when I did, the armholes looked like I could have shoved my entire body through them, they were so huge. Was I really that big only five months back?

Still, I wasn't complaining too much, I'd lost something like 30 inches from my body by that stage. I simply decided that there was no point in buying any more clothes until I'd finally reached my target, and I still had three stone to go.

* * *

In August 2011 Steve and I were going to be celebrating our fifteenth wedding anniversary. I wasn't sure yet exactly how we would be celebrating, but I certainly wasn't expecting what happened next! At work one day I got a text from Steve. He'd seen a photo of me on the red carpet at the soap awards (there must have been quite a few – I was on it for long enough!). Seemingly, though, this one was rather good. Steve's text said: *Wow! You look fantastic. I could marry you all over again.* Well, before we knew it we were having serious conversations about doing just that: renewing our wedding vows. We were both really struck with the idea and decided to go for it. For me, it wasn't just about being able to get into a nice size 16 frock and have a good party; it was much deeper than that. We'd been through a lot together over those fifteen years and that to me was something to celebrate. When I'd had my hip replacement, Steve literally did everything for me: school runs, shopping, cleaning (the house was always immaculate) as well as running a demanding business. It had been the same when I'd broken my arm over Christmas; Steve was there to help me with every boring little chore. And I'd been away from home so much in the past year working on *Emmerdale*, which many couples would have struggled with. For us, though, things had never been better, and we both knew how lucky we were to have one another.

For me the vow renewal was also about celebrating a new phase in my life. I'd had a fantastic experience working on *Emmerdale* and rediscovered my passion for acting; I'd committed to the LighterLife programme and stuck to it. I was changing my body and the way I thought about food, and best of all I had set out to achieve a goal that was so very important to me, and I *was* achieving it so far. Now I had something else to plan and look forward to.

We set the date for 6 August and I was really hoping that I might be as near as damn it at my target weight by that point: 11 stone. Blimey, 11 stone, I could hardly imagine it. Was that those flamin' angels I could hear singing again? Once we'd decided to go ahead with the vow renewal ceremony, Steve decided to have a crack at LighterLife himself. We also had a holiday in Mallorca coming up, so that was another little incentive for him to get rid of a few pounds. Of course, he didn't have anywhere near the amount of weight to lose that I did, so the regime I was on was much too drastic. He was a bit overweight, however, so he decided to go on what's called LighterLife 'Lite'. This meant having three packs a day instead of four, and then a healthy, low calorie meal in the evening. Still no booze and chocolate though, oh no! It's something you have to stick to just as rigidly if you want the results. The thing is, it doesn't matter whether you've got eight and a half stone to lose, or half a stone, it's still a goal you set yourself, and it requires the same amount of discipline – just for a shorter length of time.

At this point I was asked if I would do an interview with *Woman* magazine. Doing publicity and interviews that help promote *Emmerdale* is all part and parcel of working on the show, and all of the actors do it. I guess after seeing me on the red carpet at the soap awards they were also interested in how I'd lost all the weight and what I was doing to keep it off and what have you. In any case I was glad to do it. They wanted to do a photoshoot too, including a shot for the front cover. How very nice, I thought. I'll be a cover girl at last!

Now usually at photoshoots of any sort in the past I'd been more often than not underwhelmed by the outfits on offer. I particularly remember the publicity shoots we used to do when I was on *Birds of a Feather*. Lesley, Linda and I would all turn up at the studios on the morning of the shoot, and it would always be the same story. There would be a clothes rail as long as the Great Wall of China for Lesley because she was a tiny little thing (I think she'd have been a size 6 or an 8). Then there'd be a fairly reasonable-sized rail of clothes for Linda, who must have been around a size 10. Then there would be two old blouses thrown over a hanger on the back of a door for Pauline. There was never anything for me to choose from and the funny thing about it, looking back, is that I wasn't even that big then. Yes, I was bigger than the other two girls but I was hardly Godzilla, for God's sake. So back then I'd just go through the motions, wear whatever it was the stylist had picked out for me, have my picture taken and then go home. So, no, photoshoots had never been one of my favourite things and I'd never looked forward to them with any sort of enthusiasm. I suppose this was one of the reasons I had no real interest in clothes or fashion back then. There never seemed to be much point.

When I walked into the photoshoot for *Woman* magazine, however, it was a whole different ball game. As usual there was a stylist and make-up artist, and to be honest I was quite looking forward to being made up, as my character in *Emmerdale*, Hazel, hadn't worn the slightest scrap of make-up for months. We'd decided that it was right for the character, given her miserable disposition during the assisted suicide storyline. So if anyone says to you that Pauline Quirke looked a bit ropey during some of her *Emmerdale* scenes, you can tell them, yes, that's because she was the only actress on British television not wearing any bloody make-up! Put that in your pipe! Anyway, back to the photoshoot.

There was a lovely lady called Jilly waiting for me whom I'd spoken to on the phone about sizes and colours, and from what I could see, a really gorgeous selection of colourful clothes was ready for me to try on, too. This was a complete revelation, I can tell you. I mean we're talking about a woman who previously thought that the only reason you wore clothes was because if you didn't you'd get arrested. But once I started looking through these clothes, it was mind-blowing. There was a gorgeous floral-print top, an entire white ensemble that was very pretty, and there was even a long leopard-print dress with a light denim jacket to go over it.

Blimey, they ain't got that for me, have they? That was my initial thought when I spotted it. Animal print?

I just couldn't imagine it.

The first outfit I tried on after I'd had my hair and make-up done, though, was a cerise pink silk blouse with a softer pink pair of trousers, which everyone agreed looked very nice. I didn't really feel like looking in the mirror at that point because I was still a bit daunted by the whole thing, so I just leaned against the back of a pink sofa, ready for my first shots of the day. Now although I felt reasonably relaxed, I do have to be careful when I'm in front of a camera, smile-wise, because if I show too much teeth I tend to have a look of Shergar. As it was, everyone was happy with the set-up so off we went. After clicking away happily for a while the photographer, David Venni, asked me if I'd like to have a look at one of the pictures.

'No, it's all right,' I said. 'I'll wait and see it when I buy the magazine, don't worry.'

'No, please, have a look,' he said. 'I'd like you to see one.' Then he turned his iPad towards me so I could see the shot and my mouth fell open.

'Is that me?' I said nervously. 'Have you touched that up?'

I seriously didn't know who it was I was looking at for a moment.

'No, I haven't touched it up,' he said. 'It's all you.'

I suddenly felt a lump rise in my throat and tears stinging my eyes. That pretty girl on the screen really was me.

I felt like I was watching an episode of *10 Years Younger* when they turn the mirror round to reveal somebody's miraculous makeover and everyone screams with delight. I didn't scream, though. I could barely even speak.

As the day went on, I eventually tried on the leopard-print dress, topped off with amber and gold-coloured jewellery and some high-heeled gold sandals. When I did finally look in the mirror I thought: Wow! Yeah! For a start the dress actually fitted, which is always a result in my book, but also it looked really, really lovely. It's strange, I was seeing with my own eyes what I looked like, but I still couldn't quite grasp the fact that it was actually me I was looking at. I somehow didn't quite recognize the person in front of me. Still, I hadn't spent the last thirty years staring into mirrors so I don't see me spending any more time doing it now, but it was certainly a strange moment or two standing there – strange and wonderful.

I thought about the old me during photo-sessions past, not even vaguely interested in what I was wearing and telling the stylist, 'Yep! Put me in whatever you want. As long as it ain't got a stain down it, I'll wear it!'

That was my idea of fashion back then, but hopefully from now on that attitude will be a thing of the past. I truly loved the experience that day, and it was so lovely to feel that good and look it too.

When the pictures came out in *Woman* a couple of weeks later they were syndicated everywhere. Apparently there was some little news story about a phone-hacking scandal that week, but you might have missed it under the deluge of stories about Pauline Quirke's remarkable weight loss. Or not! I was getting texts and calls from the world and its wife telling me they'd spotted the new pictures of me in this paper or that magazine, and how wonderful they were. Something had changed. This was no longer poor put-upon Hazel of *Emmerdale* looking stressed and drawn with no make-up on and wearing a poncho. This was fifty-two-year-old former 'fat actress' Pauline Quirke, looking better than she ever dreamed possible. Happy days!

10

From Arsonist to Second Whore

As the year trundled on into summer, work on *Emmerdale* was as busy as ever. Hazel was now in the midst of a court case for helping poor Jackson off himself and so I got to wear a hell of a lot of black, which was very flattering I must say. Following the trial, Hazel was then off to Morocco, which meant I got to look a bit more healthy and bronzed when I came back on screen. I think I was lucky with the storylines I had and, when I eventually left the show at Christmas, it was great that the door was left open for me to return if I wanted to.

I knew I was really going to miss the cast when I left. If you were going to be away from your family for lengthy periods of time, the *Emmerdale* cast were great people to be spending that time with. I would particularly miss my friends Charley and Lucy, who were a constant source of fun and support. At about that time Lucy did an interview in a magazine and mentioned how close she and I had become, which was very touching. Mind you, she said I was just like a mother to her – cheeky cow! Wait till I see her, I thought, when I read the article. But then again, I suppose I could just about be her mother, age-wise, but she could at least have said older sister!

A few people asked me why I'd decided to leave *Emmerdale* if I loved it so much. Well, *Emmerdale* is in Leeds and my family are in Buckinghamshire, and at the end of the day my family mean more to me than any job. Leeds is a fair old trot from Buckinghamshire, and eighteen months living mostly away from home and playing the same character is long enough, I reckon.

That being said, I think that the role of Hazel Rhodes has probably been the one that sums me up, as an actress and as a person, more than any other. I suppose it's because she's a mother, first and fore-most, and that's how I see myself: as a mother and a wife. Being an actress comes third. In Hazel's story-line her life was her child, like mine is my kids, and

I was very aware of that while I was playing her. Of course, Hazel is just one in a long line of different types of women I've played over the years.

As many of you may know, I've been acting since I was knee high to a grasshopper: since the age of nine, in fact, when in 1968 I joined a drama club simply because I had a wart on my hand. It's true! There were two after-school clubs at Ecclesbourne Primary School in Islington: one was drama and the other was country dancing. Well, I had a wart on my finger so nobody wanted to hold my hand, which made country dancing a definite no-no. So I joined the drama club, which was set up by a lady called Anna Scher in the school's art room, and ran for an hour and a half after school twice a week. I remember there being quite a few kids there that first week, including my future screen sister, Linda Robson, and Ray Burdis, who went on to become a well-known actor and film producer. I just thought it would be fun, and once I got into the swing of it, acting was something I felt very comfortable doing. It was all improvisation work – on our own or in groups, so we'd all sit in a big circle and Anna would give us a topic, a theme, or a first line. Then it was up to each person or small group to come up with a piece of theatre to perform in front of the rest of the

club members. The focus was on a natural performance, and a natural voice. It was up to us to tell
a story the way we wanted to tell it. As a lot of the
kids in the club weren't the greatest readers in
the world, Anna felt that scripts might be inhibiting
for some people, but improvisation really worked
for everyone.

By 1970, Anna's drama club had proved
extremely popular, and the art room in our school
simply wasn't big enough, so she found a place in a
community hall in a block of flats called Bentham
Court, which was just across the road. This was a
much bigger space, and we were able to use it from
4.30 pm till 6 – after that it was bingo. The funny
thing was that the bingo ladies always turned up
early, so we usually had an audience for the last half-
hour. The old girls sat in the back, rabbiting, while
we all acted our little hearts out. It was a brilliant
start for me and I think I was very lucky to have
been in that original group. By 1975, Anna had
about 1,000 pupils, plus 5,000 more on the waiting
list.

Up until that time, kids who wanted to act had to
apply and audition for a stage school, like Italia
Conti or the Barbara Speake Stage School, and these
were the places where all the casting agents and

directors would find young actors and new talent. As Anna's drama club grew, though, word got around about how good it was, and pretty soon we had directors and casting agents coming to watch us perform too. We didn't do special performances for them: anyone who came would just sit at the back and observe our normal drama club classes; it was a sort of open audition for all of us.

It was from one of these open auditions that I got my first proper acting break, in a show called *Dixon of Dock Green*, which was a series about a good old British bobby called George Dixon. In it I played a young girl who liked to set fire to things. That was my first time in a television studio and to me it was something wonderfully different: something exciting in comparison with just going to school every day. However, even though I was very young, Anna had instilled in me that when I was at the studio I was there to do a job. Acting was great fun, yes, but it was also a job of work, and I had to remember that. It was an adult environment and I wasn't there to muck about. I had to learn my lines and do as I was told, and I had to be well mannered at all times. She was quite a disciplinarian.

To be honest, I wouldn't have got away with much anyway, what with my mum there as my chaperone. Oh yes! If you were under sixteen, you had to have a chaperone while you were working – that was one of the many rules for child actors then. You were also only allowed to work for fifty-four days in any year, and half a day counted as a whole one. For the other half of the day you'd be at school, or you'd have lessons from a private tutor, and if shooting hadn't finished by seven o'clock, it was tough. An official from County Hall would magically appear, tap his watch, and then the chaperone would be told to take you off home. It didn't matter whether the director hadn't finished all of his shots for the day. In fact, every time you were offered an acting job you had to go to County Hall with your parents to apply for a licence, and if you'd done more than the allowed fifty-four days that year, you wouldn't get the licence even if you'd got the part! It was all strictly regulated, and still is today.

On the whole, I remember everyone being very kind and patient with me when I did that first job, including the lovely director, a man called Robin Nash, so to me it was a fantastic experience. At the time I don't think I truly grasped the magnitude of what it meant to be appearing on television, or acting professionally. For me, as I said, it was just something different, a break from the norm, and I loved doing it.

I do sometimes wonder what would have happened if all those grown-ups on the set of *Dixon* hadn't been as lovely to me as they were when I was a nine-year-old. Would I have carried on acting if I'd had a bad experience? Probably not: but I'm glad I did. I'm certainly glad I knocked on the staff-room door at Ecclesbourne Primary School that day and asked Anna if I could join the new drama club. It was a life-changing moment for me. And because of that moment, and because I enjoyed the club so much and was lucky enough to get that first job with a great group of people, my life veered off on a totally different route. There wouldn't have been a hope in hell of my mum being able to afford to send me to a drama school. People like me, and the other kids at Anna's club with a similar background, simply didn't become famous actors. It just didn't happen. Sure, you had a few success stories: the working-class heroes of the 1960s, like Michael Caine, for example, but they were very few and far between. In those days, acting was still a middle-class profession, and I believe people like Anna helped change all that.

It's the main reason why Steve and I decided to

start up our own drama academies all round the country. The idea that some kid from Newcastle or Brixton (or wherever we may be) might pop along to one of our drama groups and change their life for the better is why we set them up in the first place. In fact, I'm proud to say we've now got one little fourteen-year-old girl from Kent who has landed a major role in *EastEnders*. And as happy as I am for her, I just want her to have a good time, like I did on my first job.

Once I'd done *Dixon* I started auditioning for more parts, and I found myself playing all manner of troubled children. In 'Eleanor', which was a BBC *Play for Today*, I played a withdrawn child who goes missing (this also starred my drama-club mate, Ray Burdis), and in *Jenny Can't Work Any Faster* I played a young autistic girl whose dad is worried about her being . . . you guessed it . . . withdrawn! I was obviously terribly good at 'withdrawn' at that age. Looking back, I suppose it all sounds amazing, too good to be true, but at the time it didn't feel like that at all. There were a lot of young people from Anna's club, like Linda and Ray, doing the exact same thing as I was, and I took it in my stride back then – even the auditions. I really did just think of acting as a job that I'd been lucky enough to have the chance to do. It wasn't about being rich, it wasn't about being a star: it was just what I did. And, as I say, it was only fifty-four days a year at most. The rest of the time I was going to school, playing with my friends, doing homework or running errands for my mum, just like any other kid. Mind you, I'm not saying that acting wasn't hard work at times, either: you really had to knuckle down and learn your lines if you didn't want to get told off by a director, and sometimes there was a lot of hanging about, too. If you didn't have a major role and lots to do on any given production, it could get quite boring for a kid. I always had a book on the go while I was working.

By the time I was a teenager in the mid-1970s I was the host of several different kids' TV shows: *You Must Be Joking, Pauline's Quirkes* and then *Pauline's People*, as well as acting in TV shows like *The Duchess of Duke Street*, *Angels*, and films like *The Elephant Man* with John Hurt, where I played Second Whore!

It's been a varied career, thus far. In fact, the thing I most enjoy about acting is that I've been able to play both sides of the coin, with comedy and drama. Yes, I suppose during and after *Birds of a Feather* people saw me primarily as a comedy actress, but then I did *The Sculptress*, a drama about a woman called Olive Martin who was imprisoned for the murder of her mother and sister, and since then I've played as many dramatic roles as I have funny ones.

The Sculptress really was a high point for me and I'm dead proud of it. The part of morbidly obese prisoner Olive Martin couldn't have been more different from that of cheeky Sharon Theodopolopodous from *Birds*, and at the time I thought it was quite brave casting on the part of the producers. After all, I was in one of the BBC's most watched comedy shows, and suddenly I was cast in a major dramatic role that was extremely dark. Not only that, but on one of the nights on which *The Sculptress* was screened, there was also an episode of *Birds of a Feather*. I remember thinking, Oh God! Is anyone going to believe me as Olive right after watching me in *Birds*? Are the viewing figures going to drop? Fortunately, it made absolutely no difference at all, and *The Sculptress* was a big success. I was thrilled at the reaction I got to the portrayal of Olive, and so happy that people found it utterly believable that I could be both Sharon and Olive. With Olive, I'd just done what I always did: I tried to make it look as if I wasn't acting. That's my goal with every role, really, to try my best to be as natural as possible, so that the audience can forget that I'm playing a part. Of course, it's a bit tougher to achieve when you're playing a serial killer or the like, but I still try to apply the same principle. With Hazel, I was playing drama and comedy all in one role, and I guess that's why I loved it so much.

That said, I'm not one of those actors who prepare for their upcoming roles by doing lots of research on any particular subject. I don't get involved in the analysis of a character more than I feel is necessary. With Hazel, for instance, I didn't feel that I needed to go off and research the issue of people who are fighting for the right to die, I just acted on instinct, as you would have to if that sort of situation was thrown at you. Marc Silcock, however, did have to research his part as he was playing a tetraplegic and, of course, he wanted to get it exactly right. Even when I've played a nurse or some other medical role in the past, I never took myself off to a hospital to see how it was all done. There are always medical advisers on set to show you how any procedures should be performed, and that's enough for me. I knew all the most important things about working as a nurse anyway, like folding perfect corners when making a hospital bed: I learned that from being on a TV show, *Angels*!

I was offered the chance to research the part of a character in more depth when I did a TV drama alongside Ray Winstone, called *Our Boy*. I played a woman called Sonia, whose only son is killed in a hit and run accident. During the making of the programme I was presented with the opportunity of speaking to parents who had been through child bereavement, and listening to their experiences. I wouldn't do it, though. I just couldn't sit there for two hours talking to people who had really lost a kid, simply because their tragedies might help me with an acting part. I couldn't even begin to imagine or absorb the kind of loss they would have suffered. I'd surely be insulting them. I felt exactly the same about the 'right to die' storyline in *Emmerdale*. My job, as an actress, is to pretend, and to make it as real as I can – and that's all there is to it.

Before I did *The Sculptress* I'd read the book, but it was quite different from the screenplay we worked from for the film. With roles like that I let the appearance of the character lead me as much as anything. Olive was quite an extreme-looking character, so on *The Sculptress* I collaborated with the make-up and costume people about how she might look, move and even speak, and that all helped. I had a cast made for a fat suit, and I wore hair extensions, so by the time the costume and make-up people had finished with me and I looked in the mirror . . . well, I just didn't look like me any more. That drastic transformation really helped me with my portrayal, and the rest is simply down to good old-fashioned acting! Using all those skills I learned years ago at Anna Scher's drama club, and taking on a character to the point where you don't feel like you're acting it any more. In fact, the greatest compliment anyone can pay me is to tell me, 'It's like you're not acting, Pauline!' Then I know I've done my job.

I never go to advance screenings to watch my work, though. I can't bear having loads of other people around when I see myself on screen in something new for the first time. What if they all think I'm crap? What if people don't laugh when I'm being funny, or do laugh when I'm not? No, I'd much rather be in my own front room, watching it on my TV, surrounded by the people who love me.

11

Return of the Seatbelt

As Hazel was off on holiday to Morocco, it meant that Pauline was getting a holiday as well. Hurrah! Steve and I were off to Mallorca for a week and I couldn't wait.

Holidays have always been such an important thing for me, Steve and the kids, especially with my work schedule being as full-on as it has been over the years. I believe that one good two-week holiday a year is a must – if you're able to afford it – so that's what we always try to achieve. Like many parents, I want my kids to do the things I never could when I was growing up, and holidays were certainly not on the agenda when I was little, I can tell you. I simply didn't have any childhood holidays. My mum would have to save for weeks just to give me and my brother and sister a day out at the seaside every now and then because she could never have afforded an entire week away; but we appreciated those days out just as if they *were* a holiday. My mum's favourite seaside spot was Walton-on-the-Naze, which is a small coastal town in Essex, just north of Clacton. Getting on the train was an adventure in itself, and when we got there we'd play on the beach, eat fish and chips, and go on all the kids' fun-fair rides. Even back then we knew that my mum would've had to really stretch her budget to take us all out, but to be honest, we didn't know any kids who went on posh holidays. Hardly anyone went abroad back in the 60s – well, certainly not the people we knew, so I guess we didn't know what we were missing.

I think my first real holiday experience was going to the Isle of Wight with the school, and it wasn't a pleasant one. It was a class trip in my last year of primary school, so I guess I would have been about 11. My mum would have paid a couple of shillings a week over the year so that I could go, bless her, but I absolutely hated it. I'm sure it was a two-week trip, or if it wasn't it flippin' well seemed like it was – it was vile! Don't get me wrong, I'm not blaming the Isle of

Wight itself, but that trip was one of the worst experiences of my young life. First time away from my mum, somewhere I didn't like, doing stuff I didn't enjoy with a bunch of teachers who were absolute gits! I was really miserable by the time I got home, I can tell you, and I've never been back to the Isle of Wight since.

I think that's why a good family holiday is such an important thing for me now. I just didn't have them when I was younger. By the time I first took my Emily away on holiday, aged six, it was to Disneyland in Florida, and since having Charlie we've been on lots of great trips, including a few Caribbean cruises, which we all loved. For me it's about the family being away together having a good time, wherever that may be.

On this particular holiday, however, the thing I was most excited about was the flamin' seatbelt actually going round me, and not having to ask a stewardess the dreaded 'Have you got an extension belt?' question. In fact, as I walked down the aisle of the plane I thought about some of the other times I'd made that same short journey towards my seat: filled with anxiety, and terrified that the seatbelt wasn't going to fit. When I eventually sat down next to Steve, I tentatively took hold of the seatbelt and clicked it into place. Then I unclicked it and clicked it in again, and then again, and then again. Wow! I'm surprised I didn't break it, to be honest; I clicked the bloody thing in and out so many times! Let's face it, folks, the seatbelt debacle had been a terrible 'light bulb above the head' moment for me back when it wouldn't even stretch round me, and now here I was with the little clasp clicking in and out with the greatest of ease. To me, the sound of that clicking belt was the most fantastic, brilliant thing ever. I put it on, I took it off, I put it on, and I took it off: and each time it still went round me effortlessly – marvellous! I imagined new scenarios now – an announcement on the plane's public address system perhaps: 'Could the lady in seat number 36C please keep her flamin' seatbelt done up!'

To top it all, there was even some slack. Yes, seat-belt slack!

'Should we get the extension belt now?' Steve joked.

That's when it hit me: we really didn't have to. And I began to cry.

Other novelties on this noteworthy plane journey included the little fold-away table going right down flat instead of resting on my tummy at half-mast, and my feet not swelling up to the size of balloons.

I was crossing and uncrossing my legs like a mad thing, simply because I hadn't been able to do it before. If all that weren't enough to make me want to reach my target and then keep that weight off, then nothing ever would be.

Once we were in Mallorca and at the hotel, there were even more new treasures to uncover. Instead of skulking on the balcony in my swimming costume, I was unashamedly down at that swimming pool strutting my stuff with all and sundry. Of course, I wasn't flaunting myself, no, nor was I exhibiting all my bits and pieces in a tiny little bikini. That would have been upsetting for everyone! I was, however, sporting a brand new bathing costume and I didn't even put a flaming cardigan over the top of it. I also didn't feel the compulsion to do my usual hundred-yard dash from the sun lounger to the pool so that no one had a chance to gawp at me. It was a really good feeling, to be honest: not something I sat and thought about for the entire holiday, of course, but lovely nonetheless. I didn't have to endure that familiar grey cloud of self-consciousness hovering above me, and I didn't need to layer myself in long T-shirts and oversized tops to cover up in the baking heat. I was just a normal woman lying by the pool in a swimming costume – just like everyone else. It was really rather nice!

Before we'd actually left for Mallorca I'd made an important decision. I'd decided to test myself, an experiment if you like, with me as the guinea pig. I'd decided to go on to LighterLife Lite whilst on my holiday. This meant having three packs a day instead of four, and one proper meal in the evening: that's right, folks – real food! (Ooh! I can hear those gasps from here.) Now, this is something you're not advised to do while on 'total'. You're supposed to stay on the total plan until you are right down to your target weight, mine being 11 stone. Total is total, and that is that. You're in abstinence. I knew that my LighterLife counsellor would not have approved of this experiment, and I knew that I was taking a risk trying it, but I wanted to test myself. I'm a stubborn cow like that.

Still, there was no small amount of trepidation involved with this decision, but niggling doubts aside, I felt pretty confident that I, Pauline Quirke, would be able to make level-headed food choices and still keep on losing weight during my holiday. The other thing that I feel I must point out is that going on to the 'light' plan wasn't in any way a 'reward' for my recent hard work and dieting diligence. It's when you start looking at food as a reward, like I'd done so often in the past, that you're in big trouble. You know the drill: Pauline, you've worked so hard today, you deserve something from the Ginsters range, accompanied by a fine salted snack, all washed down with a large glass of something Spanish, etc., etc., etc.!

Anyway, I certainly wasn't going to cock up all the good work I'd done – no, sir! And there were to be no cheeky glasses of sangria while I was flicking through my Martina Cole by the pool, or even a white wine spritzer to wash my dinner down either: there was no grey area there – no alcohol! Still, I was confident that I could do it. I'd have my three packs during the day, and a small, sensible meal in the evening. YOU CAN DO IT, PAULINE! I was feeling strong.

The food at our hotel was served as a buffet, so there were myriad choices. I was happy about that, though, as it meant that I could choose what I put on the plate rather than ordering something that looked innocuous on a menu, but ultimately came with a hitherto unmentioned buttery sauce and a molehill of fried potatoes masquerading as veg. On the first evening Steve and I walked into the restaurant, the buffet table seemed like it was 50ft long and positively groaning under the weight of its delicious-looking load. Desserts, cheeses . . . it was all there . . . waiting . . . tempting. Now it was up to me. I'd had my three packs that day, where every single calorie was counted out for me, and now it was my choice. I had to decide. The first thing I realized was that I didn't want meat – I just didn't fancy it – but there was some lovely freshly grilled fish on offer. I plumped for two small fillets with a bit of salad – no dressing – and sat down at the table. Well, when I put that forkful of fish into my mouth I can honestly say that I felt like I'd tasted fish for the first time in many, many years. I really felt the flavour – and it was absolutely beautiful!

'Of course it was beautiful, Pauline,' I hear you all cry. 'You hadn't eaten for over six months, you silly mare!'

No. It was more than that. I really was savouring the flavour of something delicious – and healthy – that I'd chosen to eat: not just put in my mouth and then washed down with a glass of Viña Sol. It was a whole new experience.

As I said, alcohol wasn't part of the deal anyway, and neither was the 'crooked thinking' that I'd become all too fond of in ye olden days. It's something we discussed quite a lot in the counselling sessions, 'crooked thinking'. An example of this would have been something like: Ah! You've only had a bit of fish and a bit of salad, girl, a bit of cake won't hurt, will it? YES! Yes, it will hurt! It's not even about how many calories might be in that piece of cake, it's about me moving the goalposts and that's a rocky road I've been down once too often. So whereas before I might have been tempted to go down to breakfast the next morning and have a poached egg on toast (why not? You did great last night with the fish, it won't hurt, etc.), *this* time I was straight back on my porridge pack in the morning. *This* time I was remembering how serious and dangerous my problem was before I started this eating plan, however good I felt now. Funny though, I did worry slightly when I was having my packs at the table during breakfast and lunch, that people coming after me might wonder what the white powder all over the table was. The porridge pack was white powder; the shepherd's pie was white powder. You can just imagine it, can't you?

''Ere, I think that Pauline Quirke's a bit of a coke-head, Ethel!'

The experiment lasted five days, and as soon as I got back from holiday, I was straight back on to 'total'. It's not something I would necessarily encourage, though, testing yourself like that, but it's something I needed to do for me. That week I lost five and a half pounds.

It wasn't only the swimsuit and the food choices that changed while we were away on holiday, either: the activities portion of our holiday altered drastically, too, and for one simple reason . . . I wanted to walk! Mallorca is such a gorgeous place, and to me it has everything. At one time we'd been lucky enough to own a villa there, but on this occasion we were staying at a hotel in Palma. Now Palma, like many beautiful cities, is all about walking, and previously this was something that hadn't been easy for me because of my size. Still, there I was thoroughly enjoying exploring the city on foot, and for hours at a time, too! We walked all round the magnificent Cathedral of Santa Maria, which is all steps and steep climbs, and I loved it. This would have been virtually impossible before. We'd never have gone for long walks, and I would have had to plan how far it was to walk to this place or that to make sure I could manage it. Being lighter made a huge difference to my holiday, which was fantastic. I do love Mallorca, and I don't think I'll ever get bored with it.

I made a trip to the gym every day too – just

because I wanted to and I felt like I could manage the exercise. There was less of me, let's face it, and so it was a damned sight easier. When there was 19 stone 6 of me I was exhausted after about five minutes; now, I was feeling a lot more confident about it.

Bewilderingly, I'd become more and more attracted to the exercise side of things as time went on and the weight dropped off, and it became glaringly apparent that diet and exercise really did have to go hand in hand. You simply couldn't have one without the other. I'd already joined a gym in Leeds, and I was surprised to find how much I actually enjoyed it. Weird, huh?

'It's all right if you can afford a gym,' someone sniped to me after I started going. 'Not everyone can.'

'Well, if you can't afford it 'ave a run round the block, love,' was my reply. We can all find excuses not to do something. I knew that better than anyone.

I had more energy in the evenings and more time too. I wasn't cooking myself meals, and during the summer I couldn't sit outside the pubs drinking Sauv Blanc with all the other revellers, so I just sort of found myself plodding away at the gym. Then after six gym visits I'd treat myself to something nice, like a manicure or fancy pedicure and a bright shade of nail varnish. That was my reward for exercising: prostitute toenails!

Once we got back from holiday I even went to Gap in Leeds with Emily, just to treat myself to a couple of bits. Nothing that exciting, I was on an expedition for a hooded fleece. I'd previously only ever been in Gap to buy stuff for the kids, as there'd been nothing even approaching my size. Now, though, here I was holding up a blue and white striped hoodie: pleasant, but a little on the small side.

'That's nice, Mum!' Emily enthused.

'But I need an adult one, love,' I said. 'We're in the children's section. Let's see if they've got it in my size.'

'Mum, this is the ladies' section, not the kids',' Emily laughed. 'And that top *is* your size now.'

And blow me, it was!

I even went mad and decided I might try out a few new methods of exercise that I couldn't have contemplated when I was 19-plus stone. I bought a book entitled *Pilates*, thinking it was a new discipline I might like to attempt. After all, I'd heard great things about it from quite a few people, so why not have a stab at it myself? When I got the book home, though, I noticed with some concern that the guy on the cover was the actor Ross Kemp. Bizarre, I thought, popping on my reading glasses – I never had Ross down as the Pilates type. But with glasses on and eyes now focusing I spotted the title above the picture. Oops! What I'd actually purchased was *Pirates* by Ross Kemp.

12

Renewal

We must have made a rather large carbon foot-print on the day of our wedding vow renewal, I'm slightly ashamed to say. There were people trotting in from all over the globe. Friends from San Francisco and from Spain, not to mention all the people who came down to Beaconsfield from Yorkshire to be with us – the *Emmerdale* crowd. Lucy Pargeter was there with her husband and little girl; Zoe Henry and Jeff Hordley, who are a real-life married couple, were there too, as was Danny Miller and one of our directors, Mike Lacey, who was with his partner, Cheryl. Charley Webb and her partner, Matthew, who plays David Metcalfe in *Emmerdale*, had driven all the way from Edinburgh just to be there too. So all in all there was a fairly substantial *Emmerdale* turnout. Of course this meant that Steve's mum, bless her, wanted photos with some of the cast. Not all of them, mind you, just some of them.

'I want a picture with that one and that one. No, not that one, that one,' she said, pointing at gorgeous Danny as if she could pick and choose.

There were eighty guests in total, all coming to celebrate with me, Steve and the kids. I was really excited about it.

We had the ceremony, and the subsequent party, at home in our garden, because that's where we're most comfortable, and I had busily planned and ordered most of what we needed for the day while I was up in Leeds: on the internet, if you don't mind, Googling away on my new iPad! (It's all very new to me, ordering things online, to be honest. I recently ordered a pair of black jeans online from John Lewis, which was rather elating, especially as they were a size 14 and actually fitted when I went to collect them.) Anyway, I'd done most of the preparation up front, which left me quite relaxed about the whole affair. I've got to a point in my life when I want to avoid getting stressed out if at all possible. Ultimately it never helps, does it? So the marquees went up, the bouncy castle went up (that was for the children, not us) and everything was hunky-dory.

Looking out of my window as I got ready, I could see the weather wasn't as great as I'd have hoped for at the start of August, but at least it wasn't pelting down with rain. Fortunate, that was, as I was wearing cream silk shoes and a dress I'd bought from Phase Eight, which was also a beautiful cream (well, let's face it, a white dress would have been strongin' it a bit, do you know what I mean?). Still, the dress was lovely, but only just about did up at the back, bringing me to the conclusion that I'd been slightly optimistic about the size – I definitely could have gone one up. It was also a bit long when I bought it, but the lovely ladies at the *Emmerdale* costume department had kindly taken it up for me.

Once I'd got the dress on I felt really lovely. I couldn't have worn this or anything like it six months ago, I thought. What a difference. It did take me a while to fathom out what the crunching noise was every time I walked across the room, but then on closer inspection I realized the fabric was covered in sequins around the bottom and I was, in fact, stepping on them with every move. Steve, on the other hand, had insisted he wear the suit he got married in fifteen years ago. 'You've spent so much on your dress,' he said to me, 'I'll have to wear my wedding suit to balance it out.' Following his little foray into the wonderful world of weight loss, it actually fitted him with no problem. In fact, it was a bit too big!

I'd plumped for no make-up on the day, knowing I was likely to spend most of the day crying, because I do tend to weep at the drop of the proverbial hat: especially if it's something to do with my kids, who were taking part in the ceremony. Ray Winstone once called me a 'water cart' years ago, because of my tendency to blub all the time – and at almost any-thing – and I suppose that moniker has sort of stuck with me.

The guests were arriving at 3 pm and Steve came to escort me down from the house to the marquee at 4 pm for my big moment. And when he told me I looked beautiful, I knew full well that he would have told me that even if I hadn't lost all the weight, and he'd have meant it, too. That's one of the things I love most about Steve: he loves me for me, not my body shape. He was happy that I'd lost weight because it made *me* happy, and if I hadn't lost it he wouldn't think of me as any less beautiful than he did on that day.

One of the other great things about my relation-ship with Steve is that we think so much alike. Even during the planning stages of the vow renewal, we'd been on the exact same wavelength, even though I was up in Leeds and he was at home in Buckingham-shire. The celebrant who was to perform the ceremony sent both Steve and me, separately, a whole host of options for what we might want, along with reams and reams of ideas about the kinds of vows we might want to exchange. Without even consulting one another, Steve and I chose, almost word for word, exactly the same things and the same vows. It was quite amazing. Even though we each made our own separate guest list for the occasion, without exception, it was the same people we both wanted to invite. Our guest lists were like carbon copies of one another.

It's pretty much always been the same, which is why we've been able to work together so well with-out too many cross words! Steve is my agent these days, having worked in television himself for years, and I can wholly rely on him to know what I would or wouldn't be interested in doing. Of course, he'll always run things past me in an email (yes, an email: we don't sit around at home talking about work all day) but I could almost trust him to accept or turn work down on my behalf. He also knows when to admit he's wrong, and he will always go away and think about my side of any disagreement when it comes to work, or anything else for that matter.

But back to the renewal of vows. I think it's only right that a girl should make a big entrance on an occasion like this, so that's what I decided to do. As I said, the guests had arrived an hour before Steve came to collect me, so everyone was already gathered in the marquee by the time I swept through in my posh frock. When we finally walked down the aisle, with all of our friends standing up, smiling and applauding, I wasn't nervous in the least. I just felt very, very happy. Our 'wedding march' was a recording of *'Parla più piano'*, also known as 'The Love Theme from *The Godfather*', performed by Russell Watson, and it made for a wonderful moment all round. In my eyes it was absolutely perfect.

The ceremony too was gorgeous and emotional. Steve and I both lit candles from the flame of a larger candle, and then the children came forward and lit a candle each, signifying the unity of the family. Then our boy, Charlie, got up and did a beautiful reading, which, of course, set me off all over again. We do have great kids, I have to say, and it was fantastic to have Charlie, Emily and my step-daughter Lauren all there as a part of it, as well as my brother Sean and his family, and my sister Kitty, plus all Steve's family too.

In the evening we had some terrific singers performing for us; and Suzanne Shaw's husband, Jason (who is also known as JK – one half of the radio presenting duo, JK and Joel), did a DJ set for us. When we had our first dance it was to Curtis Stigers's 'You're All That Matters To Me', and we were crunching around the dance floor as we went, as another couple of hundred sequins bit the dust. Then Steve and I said a few words: no formal speeches, just off the cuff. Steve talked about my mum and his dad, who have both passed away, and how we would have loved them to be there with us, and we both relayed sincere thank-yous to everyone present, and, of course, to one another.

We had a hog roast during the evening, courtesy of the fantastic caterers from *Emmerdale*, who came all the way from Yorkshire. And yes, I did have one little slice with a bit of cucumber on the side (don't roll your eyes). I had a glass or two of wine as well, just to celebrate the occasion, but that was all. It was one special day and I was back on my packs the very next morning. After the roast pork there was chocolate mousse and a cheeseboard, and I think it was that cheese that I found the hardest to resist – but I did! I simply told myself that there was always going to be a cheeseboard, and so I had to get used to it. Anyway, I thoroughly enjoyed myself, and I tried my best to whizz around: mingling and chatting to as many people as I possibly could. I was so grateful they'd all come. The only slight downer during the evening was that I wished we'd shelled out the extra 400 quid we'd been quoted to get some bloody heaters in the marquee, as it started to get a tad nippy. As it was August, we really didn't think we'd need them, but the great British weather proved us wrong as per. By seven o'clock Charlie was dashing backwards and forwards to the house to fetch fleeces and body warmers for some of the guests, in particular the *Emmerdale* girls, who are all very slim and feel the cold a bit more. Despite this, we were up dancing for most of the night, and a marvellous time was had by all. Then, for the next day, we invited all the guests staying in nearby hotels to come back over to the house for a barbecue, which topped the weekend off beautifully.

It's funny how the whole thing came out of Steve seeing my picture in a magazine. The same woman he'd known and loved for twenty years but a lot less of her: looking glamorous and feeling good about herself. There were so many reasons to celebrate that day . . . and it was just brilliant!

13

Treats!

What did I eat when I was a kid? Did I eat too much, or too much of the wrong thing, perhaps? During LighterLife's group counselling sessions there's a lot of focus on what sort of food we ate as children, and what sort of eating habits we formed in our early years. As I said before, I sometimes get a bit worn down with all the theories and psychology surrounding the subject of food (Freud egg and chips again) but these are things I've had to address whether I liked it or not.

Now, I wasn't locked in a cupboard with a bit of stale bread as a child, nor was I malnourished, but I *was* brought up in an era when you bloomin' well ate what was put in front of you. You didn't have a choice. I don't know, maybe it was because of where I came from.

I was an ordinary kid from an ordinary background, and my mum, Hetty, brought Kitty, Sean and me up on a very restricted income. Most of the people around where we lived – Stoke Newington, East London – were like us, so I certainly didn't feel poor or deprived. In fact, there was a great feeling of community around the area we lived in. Still, people didn't have a lot of money and they couldn't afford to waste food. You certainly couldn't afford to chuck stuff away, that's for sure. We were also told to eat what we were given at school, which I would have happily chucked in the bin more often than not. I can still see the insipid, over-boiled cabbage congealing on my plate as I sat unenthusiastically at the table in the school dinner hall. A generous helping of that was enough to put me off vegetables for life; in fact I think it did put me off quite a lot of them.

At home, though, money or no money, my mum served up good, wholesome grub. As I've said before, we didn't have foreign holidays or anything like that, but there was always food on the table for my brother, my sister and me. The difference between now and back then is that if you didn't eat exactly what was put in front of you at lunchtime or at dinnertime, you went hungry. Our house wasn't filled with sweets and snacks – there was none of that frippery! Mum had a tight budget that she had to stick to and that was that. Maybe that's what's been lurking in the recesses of my mind all these years. Eat it all! Eat lots! Finish every last bit on your plate, Pauline! Who knows? Food was a big part of our lives back then, and I suppose it still is for me. Quite aside from my long-term weight problem, I actually love to feed other people. I love to cook, to entertain – and I don't see anything wrong with that. What do they call those people? Feeders? Well, that's it, then. I must be a feeder!

Luckily for us kids, my mum was a lovely cook, so I probably got my love of cooking from her. She never actually gave me step-by-step instructions on what to do or how to cook, but I suppose I just soaked up her methods and her skills as we went along. We ate the traditional meat and two veg type of suppers, not fried egg and chips – proper dinners with an abundance of vegetables. There was none of that pudding lark, though! Mum's budget couldn't stretch to puddings, so we rarely, if ever, had them. If we fancied something sweet we'd have a bit of bread and jam and that was that!

We always sat down as a family and had a big roast dinner on a Sunday, which is something I still try to insist on when I'm at home, even though my kids don't seem to be that interested. Why is it that a lot of kids don't like a Sunday roast any more? Well, mine don't anyway! Despite this, there are very few Sundays when we don't all sit down to eat together at some point during the day – even if it's not for a traditional roast lunch. Most weekends, family mealtimes are planned around Charlie's football matches or whether Emily has been out late or stayed with friends the night before; and in the summer the grub tends to be more buffet or barbecue style. But I still like us all to be together for a meal on a Sunday: it's what we did as a family when I was a child and I like the tradition of it. Of course, while I was working on *Emmerdale*, that family meal often had to be a big breakfast rather than a lunch, simply because I had to drive back up to Leeds in the afternoon. Still, that was good enough for me: as long as we were all eating around the table together.

My mum was Irish, so as well as her great roasts she baked delicious soda bread and we quite often had cheese, which, as you now know, is one of my favourite things in the entire world. An occasional treat was the fish and chip shop, but that was a bit of a luxury as it was quite expensive for us. I grew up before the takeaway generation. Back then there wasn't the plethora of fast food stores everywhere you turned. I remember when the Kentucky Fried Chicken opened in the 70s, near where we lived in Stoke Newington. Oh my God, the excitement! You'd have thought they were erecting an annex of Buckingham Palace in the high street, or the KFC counter had been crafted from pure gold, such was the brouhaha. In that era even the Wimpy Bar was an extravagance for me!

Before that it had been the Lyons Corner House, which was a chain of teashops and restaurants where my mum sometimes used to take me back in the 60s. This would be a special treat rather than an everyday occurrence, but to me it was wonderful. Every few weeks after a shopping trip – I guess I'd have been about six or seven – Mum would take me to the Lyons Corner House in Dalston, East London, for some tea and a bit of cake or perhaps a bun. Dalston was, and still is, a very big shopping area, and Saturday was the busiest shopping day of all back then. The bustling corner houses all had waitress service, with the girls decked out in smart black and white uniforms and little white hats. The restaurant windows held tantalizing displays of cakes, and the tables boasted clean white tablecloths and polished cutlery. Many of the corner houses were famous for their gorgeous art deco interiors too, so it was all dead posh – well, at least it was to me. It was a very big deal! Mum would always have a pot of tea, and I'd have an orange juice and a slice of cake, and I loved it most because it was something that my mum and me did together – just the two of us.

So no, back then there was no grabbing a quick sandwich out of Pret A Manger or a pie out of Greggs! And as for eating in the street, well, that was frowned upon. Very common indeed! When I was a kid people just didn't eat like that.

As with most people of my generation, cookery lessons at my school were the butt of many a joke. 'Home economics' they called it, and I'm sure all we did was make fairy cakes every week for five years. It wasn't really what I'd call a proper lesson, but it was part of the curriculum: girls did cooking and boys did woodwork. I don't think anyone at my school learned much in those classes. Still, as I got older my interest in food, and in cooking, grew and grew, and I started to learn things for myself. Of course, there weren't as many cookery shows on television as there are now. I mean, these days you can't flick the channel over without stumbling upon some new gastronomic virtuoso waving his spatula at you and sharing his secrets for a perfect hollandaise; but back then it was Fanny Cradock or the Galloping Gourmet, with a bit of Delia Smith if you were lucky.

There wasn't a big restaurant scene in London then either, especially in Stoke Newington. In fact, the first time I went to a proper bona fide restaurant, I was with Anna Scher, the teacher who ran the drama club I'd joined as a child. I was about ten or eleven, and Anna took a group of us kids from the drama club to a restaurant in the West End, where the only thing on the menu I recognized was a cheese salad. I remember thinking at the time: That's got to be a safe bet, I'll have that. Wrong! As it turned out, the cheese salad I was served had sultanas in it, which, for an eleven-year-old girl from the East End, was absolute culinary sacrilege. Who the hell puts flippin' fruit in a cheese salad, I wondered? What sort of sick person? I was disgusted.

When I eventually started venturing out with my mates, a typical night out might end in a kebab restaurant, or we might go for a sit-down meal at the nice Greek restaurant in Essex Road, Islington; but there still wasn't a whole lot to choose from around where I lived, so I wasn't terribly adventurous, I must say. Also, my mum expected me to be home by 10.30 each night, so I couldn't go gallivanting off to clubs and swanky restaurants up town even if I'd been inclined to – there was none of that for me back then! As I got older I did start eating in a few different restaurants and perusing menus, and I began to learn for myself what ingredients went together well, and what tantalizing new things the chefs of the day were trying out. If there was a cookery show on the TV, you would invariably find me sat in front of it. I suddenly found the subject of food fascinating.

These days I'll buy a cookery book like other people buy a novel and I love to cook and entertain for as many as you like. Whereas some people would find it a great big pain in the proverbial to whip up a sit-down supper for eight people, I find it very relaxing. Actually, it's bloody lucky I do find cookery and preparing meals so soothing, considering the fact that half the time I've got a houseful of teenage boys, what with Charlie and all his mates. I'm always roasting, baking or frying them something or other: whether it's their dinners when they come to stay over, or a few bacon rolls the next morning. In fact, some nights I'll often find myself cooking one thing for Charlie, something else for Steve and me, and then another thing for Emily. I even have a special salad just for Emily, with all her favourite things included: cheese, crispy bacon, cherry tomato, avocado, red onion and spicy chicken. It's called, appropriately enough, an Emily salad.

I enjoy it, and I love trying out recipes whenever I can. However, there are a few things that I don't think anyone should attempt to cook for themselves. I believe there's a damn good reason why God invented companies like Birds Eye and Mattessons and put them on the planet, and that's to stop us mere mortals making things like . . . hummus. I tried that once and it would have been perfectly fine had I been intending to use it to put up wallpaper, as an adhesive – or perhaps it might have made a rather sturdy putty for replacing a broken pane of glass. Edible it was not: it was a shocker!

I also tried to make panna cotta, an Italian cream dessert – Lord knows why! I first tasted it on an aeroplane and I've loved it ever since. You see, I'm one of those few, odd people who like aeroplane food. I love it! Every time that little tray is placed in front of me, there's something inside me that says: Pauline, they're giving this to you for free! How good is that? Never mind the fact that I've paid 500 quid for the flight, in my head that is still a free dinner. I even love the way it all comes in a little box covered in foil. Anyway, I digress, back to the panna cotta. I'd done everything as instructed – honestly – and then I boiled up some milk; but by the time I'd put all the ingredients together I was the proud owner of the sweetest bowl of congealed mess ever. It looked hideous! The answer is simple: don't do it. Hummus, panna cotta and lasagne (I mean, that can take hours to do, and I don't know why 'cause it's only minced beef, pasta and a bit of white sauce). Don't do it, I tell you! Let Findus do the work!

Much as I love food, these days I'm not a great one for eating out in restaurants, though I do enjoy it on special occasions. We sometimes go to Antony Worrall Thompson's restaurant in Henley-on-Thames if there's a birthday because the food is always good, and Antony is always there cooking in the kitchen himself, which makes a big difference, I think. Sometimes I find restaurants can be over-priced and in other instances disappointing – and sometimes both! It's like coffee shops. I'd never stop off at a coffee shop and pay four quid for a cup of coffee when I can be home in ten minutes and put the kettle on. Some people enjoy the experience of sitting in a restaurant or coffee shop every day, but I'm just as happy eating or drinking with family or friends at home. Plus, as I say, these days I'd rather be at home cooking something myself, like Chicken Puttanesca, which is a recent favourite of mine, or perhaps something from the fabulous Indian cookbook one of the girls from *Emmerdale* bought me for my birthday. To me, a night out at a really wonderful restaurant is a special treat, and that's how it should be.

Part of the counselling I took part in was trying to get to the bottom of some of the many issues that surround certain people's eating habits. Why do some of us love and enjoy food more than others, and when does that become a problem? (When you're tipping the scales at nearly 20 stone, that's when!) I had to look at what food meant to me, and at why I considered certain foods a treat rather than a fuel. Let's face it, it's usually the naughty calorific stuff that most of us use as a 'food treat' – so why is that? I made it quite clear to my counselling group from the outset that I had no problem about wanting to cook for, and feed, other people. Some people in the group found it difficult being around and preparing food that they couldn't then eat themselves, but I didn't. As a mother my instinct is to nurture, and part of that nurturing instinct is to feed your kids, your family. All that sat just fine with me, and would have been fine whether I was fat or thin, to be honest. However, I still came away from the counselling with plenty of food for thought (*groan*). For instance, why did I always eat in advance? Why was I always thinking that I might not get to eat later on, so I'd better have something now? I realized that for decades I'd been sort of 'stocking up' on food, just in case. What was I – a camel?

Who knows? One thing I did know was that I had to learn to separate my enjoyment of cooking from what I was putting into my own body. I had to make that work because I didn't want to give up on something I loved. I get such a buzz out of watching a chef on TV create something beautiful in the kitchen and I always will. So when people said to me – and they did – 'Oh, I could never do the sort of dieting you're doing, Pauline, because I love my food,' my answer to them was that there's a difference between loving your food and appreciating food. For me it was now about appreciating what I was eating, and trying new things that I might have not given a second thought to because I didn't view them as a treat. Fish, for example. I'd never been a fish lover: too much like hard work with all those bones; then once you've pulled it all apart you're only left with a spoonful! Now I was going to learn to appreciate fish, and try some different varieties. I had to . . . and I now wanted to. In fact, for my Christmas present I've asked Steve and the kids to book me on a cookery course with Rosemary Shrager: one that specializes in cooking fish.

I needed to start understanding and appreciating what I ate rather than just loving it. I was determined to carry on enjoying food. I just had to get the balance right.

Two rather surreal shots, both from characters' dream sequences. Preparing for the perfect dinner party as the chaotic April in *Being April* (*above*) and freezing my knickers off in Saltcoats, Scotland in *Double Nougat* (*right*).

My one and only panto season, starring as Ratbag Lady in *Dick Whittington* at the Hackney Empire with Peter Duncan and Linda in 1991.

Above: My period-drama phase, darling. Photographed by Lord Snowdon, don't you know, as Maggy in *Little Dorrit* (*above left*) with Derek Jacobi and Alec Guinness; and playing Peggotty in *David Copperfield* with James Thornton and a very young Daniel Radcliffe.

Below: With the fat suit, cast and crew of *The Sculptress* in 1997. I still think it was pretty brave of the BBC to cast me as murderess Olive Martin while I was still in *Birds of a Feather*.

Right: Filming *Down to Earth* on location in Devon. They say never work with children or animals, but I think the cow got it right first take and it was me who mucked up the shot!

Below: Looking rather stern as DCI Hazel Norton in *Cold Blood*, with Jemma Redgrave, John Hannah and Ace Bhatti.

Guess where I am? Everyone does a round of publicity shots when they join the cast of *Emmerdale*.

I was so lucky to make such good friends during my time on *Emmerdale*. Larking around off-camera with Marc Silcock and Danny Miller (*above*) and in the Woolpack with Lucy Parteger (*right*).

Below: Doing my best impression of Clint Eastwood in *A Fistful of Dollars* as I try to disguise my broken arm.

Danny, Lucy and
Charley Webb did such
an incredible job of
organizing my leaving
party: from the 'before'
and 'after' life-sized
cardboard cut-outs (*top*)
to the memory books
of my time on the show
(*bottom*), which had
me sobbing one minute
and laughing the next.

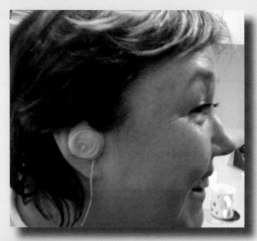

Left: Being fitted for my super-duper hearing aid. It didn't work out using it on *Emmerdale* but I'm determined to give it another go.

Below: One of our thirty Pauline Quirke Academies is based out in Majorca. On the summer break from *Emmerdale* in 2011 we went out for a visit and took the kids to see *Pirates*, a brilliant show of acrobatics and dancing.

14

The Naysayers

I have a confession to make. It's quite a big confession and perhaps I should have mentioned it earlier. I've done this all before. Yes, I did the LighterLife diet a few years back . . . and I failed. I did 100 days 'total', because that's how the programme worked back then, and following that I was supposed to go on to the 'route to management' stage. Of course, I hadn't lost anywhere near the amount of weight that I have now, but I certainly completed the first part of the regime perfectly and I shed a few stone. The problem was that I didn't do the counselling properly, so therefore didn't take time to think about why I was as fat as I was, and I stupidly decided at the end of the abstinence stage

to take a break from the programme altogether –
just for a couple of weeks. Yeah, right! I believed
that I deserved to back off from the diet for a while
because I'd been a really good girl and done the first
bit. That's the key word, 'deserve'. I'd stuck to the
diet for the allotted time, lost weight, and now I
deserved cake!

'I think I'm going to have a break for a while,' I
remember saying to my counsellor. Big mistake!
What I actually meant was, 'I've not eaten for a
hundred days, love, so I'm just popping down the
road to get some fish and chips!'

Of course, I didn't complete the counselling, I
didn't ease myself back into the deep, dark waters of
'food choice', and so I came a cropper, big time. I
never did get to the route to management stage, and
I ended up bigger than ever.

So when I started to notice a certain amount of
negativity – perhaps even disapproval – regarding
my weight loss, it began to unnerve me. At first it
was in the fairly benign form of a couple of people
coming up to me in the street or in the supermarket
– people I'd never met before – advising me that it
was time to stop.

'Oh, I think that's enough now, I don't think you
should lose any more,' one helpful lady told me.

'Well, actually, I've not reached my target yet,' I explained helpfully. 'I've got another eleven pounds to go.'

'Oh no,' she said. 'I think you're all right now, don't lose any more, you need to stop.'

There were a lot of these kinds of remarks from people, and although I started off with explanations about targets, BMI and so on, in the end I gave up. It was either that or reconcile myself to the idea that it was going to take me three hours to get round Sainsbury's every time I went in there (and God knows I have to methodically do every aisle as it is!). I knew that I hadn't reached my target and that was good enough for me.

I guess people were saying these things out of concern as much as anything else; I don't think they meant it nastily, it was their way of telling me I look all right now. There were also those, however, who thought that the type of diet I was doing was a fad, that it was unhealthy. People on forums, on Facebook, on Twitter (which I don't use myself), who said that as soon as I went back to what's considered 'normal eating', every single bit of food I ate would cling to me because I've not had it for so long. They implied that even if I only ate an ounce of cheese, I might as well have eaten 4lb of it. Well,

I'm sorry but that doesn't sound scientifically accurate to me; and, as for being unhealthy, what could be unhealthier than me as I was in January? Dr Ellie Cannon wrote in the *Daily Mail* that I would almost certainly put all the weight back on; however, she hedged her bets and suggested that I'd put it back on within the next five years. So what was she saying: that I shouldn't even try this style of diet after failing every other? Surely it's better than invasive surgery. Surely it's better to at least try. Yes, my weight was going to fluctuate once I started eating proper food again, just like anyone's does, but the only way all that weight was going to go back on was if I started eating the way I did before. I knew that!

I suppose I'd been expecting it to happen, if I'm honest. People have always got something to say, and it's usually the naysayers and worrywarts who shout the loudest.

Still, I was quite upset about the piece that a so-called celebrity columnist, who doesn't know me, wrote in a weekly magazine after seeing the pictures of me looking slimmer. I'd only just done a piece myself for the same magazine, which had been very positive with lots of nice photos of me in lovely clothes, so it was a bit of a shock, to say the least. Anyway, there I now was, splashed across the cover looking pale and drawn beneath the headline: *Pauline, stop this extreme diet now!*

Only it wasn't me in the picture looking terrible, it was me as Hazel: under TV lights with no make-up, filming what looked like an emotional scene. Of course I looked pale and drawn!

It wasn't the best of days for me to come across that article, to be honest. I always felt a little bit down when I had to tear myself away from Steve and the kids, and I was just back in Leeds after a whole month of being at home. As much as I loved the people up there, it wasn't my home. I'd also been at another photoshoot that day with lots and lots of lovely clothes, and I remember thinking that if I never saw another photo of myself ever again, it would still be too soon. I was sick of the sight of me, so I was pretty sure the British public were too. I decided then that I wasn't going to do any more of these shoots for the time being – enough was enough. I'd lost some weight, now let's move on. I was enjoying the outfits, though, that's one thing I'll never get tired of: being able to wear gorgeous clothes. Anyway, the lady from the *Emmerdale* press office got a phone call during the photo session, and she sounded a little perturbed.

'Oh really?' she was saying. 'Well, I'm with

Pauline now. Oh dear! That's not right at all, I'm disgusted.'

She eventually came over and told me about the two-page piece that this woman had written in her column and what the gist of it was: Pauline would put all the weight back on, Pauline has lost too much weight too fast, Pauline would feel a crushing failure, blah de blah! Now, the lady who had penned this article had herself had quite a public battle with weight loss. She'd lost loads of weight, done a fitness DVD or two, and then put weight back on again, so I guess she must have been thinking that I was going to do the same. Well, maybe she was right, but that didn't mean that I shouldn't try my absolute best, did it? And that's what I'd been doing.

When I'd finished the photoshoot, I drove back to my flat in Leeds, stopping at a petrol station to pick up a copy of the magazine in question. Once I was indoors, I settled down and flicked on the TV before I started to read the article, wondering just how peed off I might be once I'd read it. Within seconds of the telly coming on, however, I found myself frozen and totally horrified at what was on the screen in front of me.

There was seemingly utter chaos going on all over the country. Rioting, looting, buildings burning: it was hard to take in. I stared at the terrible pictures coming from London, and then Manchester, which wasn't all that far away from me in Leeds. What if it started here, I thought. I'm right in the centre of town; where would I go if it all kicked off around me? Perhaps I was being a bit irrational but suddenly I felt alone and vulnerable. Not being in my own home and without Steve, I was scared and I'm not afraid to admit it.

I sat back in the chair and read the magazine article to take my mind off the riots for a moment, and once I'd read it I felt even worse. I was incredibly upset by what she'd written and more than a little deflated. It's not a nice thing to have someone dismiss you so publicly, especially when you're trying to do something positive. I was pretty gutted. The combination of coming back to Leeds after a month at home, the scathing article, the long photoshoot and, of course, the terrible pictures on the news, was all a bit much in one day. Once upon a time, this would have been just the sort of thing to send me straight downstairs to the Indian for a kebab – for comfort, you know? On this occasion, however, I decided that I'd had quite enough of that particular day, and so I took myself off to bed . . . at a quarter past seven! And the funny thing was, I actually slept really well. Funny, that!

I couldn't dwell on the magazine article for too long, and after a couple of days I'd put it to the back of my mind. I had to remember, I wasn't doing this for the benefit of other celebrities or newspaper medics, and I wasn't even doing it for the public. I was losing weight for me. It was my battle, and if, ultimately, I failed, it was down to me and I was sure as hell going to go down fighting. I was determined not to become another yo-yo dieter!

Still, there were a lot of people rallying round me and supporting me too. This was posted on the LighterLife forum after the article was published:

Just read the piece in a magazine pleading with Pauline to stop the extreme dieting!! [The writer] states that once Pauline stops it will go back on. I am fizzing! Ms ***** should address her own body issues and yoyo dieting before slating LL. She is piling on the weight and is obviously plainly JEALOUS! Rant over . . . Pauline if you are reading this I hope to goodness you respond. You take no notice you are doing brilliantly!! Xx

It's stuff like that which kept me going.

Meanwhile, I was feeling really good about the gym that I'd joined at Oulton Hall in Leeds. It was very relaxed, with people of all shapes and sizes working out: not at all full of stick-thin, body-beautiful types pumping iron, clad head to toe in all the latest hi-tech gym gear. Some lovely people ran it, and I felt comfortable there doing what I had to do. With the gym being in a hotel, I even saw a guy on the treadmill in a T-shirt and pyjama bottoms one morning, which I'm sure would be frowned upon in some establishments but which I thought was quite cool. Nobody took a blind bit of notice, which is what I liked about the place. I just didn't feel self-conscious about exercising for the first time in my life. What also made me chuckle were the names of the workout machines. For instance, I enjoyed a quick blast on the 'Excite 700' of a morning: that's the name of a treadmill, just in case you were wondering.

By the start of September I was up to about 24 minutes on the running machine. I wasn't belting along, but I was going at a fair pace and going the distance. I'd also started to park my car further and further away from the gym to give myself that little bit more exercise each day. There was no doubt about it, my burgeoning enjoyment of exercise was down to the fact that I was feeling so much better about myself, so I no longer hated the thought of a gym. I was no longer this huge lump of a thing, sweating on a piece of equipment I wanted to smash, Luddite style, into small pieces – I was a fifty-two-year-old woman on a mission, armed with an iPod shuffle-nano thingy.

Yes! My kids got me all sorted out with an iPod. It was very exciting; although I was slightly troubled by some of the raunchy tunes they'd downloaded on to it for me. Popping my headphones on one morning, I was quite perturbed to find myself merrily jogging along to something that was encouraging me with the phrase, 'Rip it up, you mother*****r, rip it up!'

WHAT? Did I hear that right?

Now I have my iPod quite loud as a rule, so I had to glance round sharpish to make sure no one else was in earshot. Good grief, what on earth would people have thought? The kids, of course, denied all knowledge of any such tune when I mentioned it to them, and no doubt put it down to my slight deafness, or perhaps even a moment of bewilderment, but I was pretty sure of what I'd heard. I'd just have to wait for it to come around on the shuffle again so I could make certain.

It was funny, and quite scary, to think that when I first calculated my BMI back in January, it was about

48, which is very overweight, or obese. A good, healthy BMI is between 20 and 25; and in August 2011, eight months later, it was 26, which is still overweight, but just a little. By the end of August 2011 I weighed 11 stone 11, exactly 11 pounds away from my target weight: the target that I'd set myself back at the start. Less than a stone! Although I was very excited about the prospect of reaching that goal, there was also no small amount of trepidation involved. I was nervous! I mean, let's face it, that's where all the hard work would start, right? That's when the control would get put back into my own hands and I would have to make sure I didn't make a pig's ear of it. Up until I reached that target I'd had no food choices to make at all – apart from my little experiment on holiday. Suddenly I was going to be faced with all sorts of choices again, every day. I thought about what I would or wouldn't, or could or couldn't, eat. The naysayers were right about one thing: I couldn't go back to eating 'normal', not what I thought was normal anyway. I was going to have to rethink everything if I didn't want all this dieting to have been a complete waste of time.

I think it's safe to say that I won't ever be able to eat biscuits and cakes again. Sounds drastic, doesn't it? Surely, you'll say, a little cake doesn't hurt from time to time – but where does someone like me draw the line? When does a little cake become a lot of cake? And bread! I like bread, but the way I ate it was thick sliced and slathered with butter and a great big chunk of cheese in the middle. I can't go back to that and I don't know how I could modify it enough for it to be acceptable. I mean, how do you make a cheese sandwich that hasn't got bread or cheese in it? So I suppose I'll have to steer clear of that as well! Still, luckily for me, by the end of the summer my tastes were already changing for the better, which surprised me no end. I now loved the idea of a nice grilled fillet of fish, which I never particularly fancied before. That sounds fabulous to me – not with chips, but with a lovely fresh salad on the side and not smothered in dressing!

I'd initially been terrified of the time when I had to start making food choices every day – the route to management part of the diet – but now I was actually looking forward to it. I wanted to prove to myself, and to everyone else, that I could do it. I could make those choices. And by the end of the summer, it looked like it was going to come around sooner rather than later.

15

Stage Fright

It suddenly dawned on me that I didn't have that much time left on *Emmerdale*, and I was quite sad about it. I knew I had made the right decision, though, and the producers had informed me that they would leave the door open for Hazel to make a return, so I was fairly confident that my final scenes wouldn't see her toppling under a runaway bus, or choking to death on a cheese and tomato barm in the Woolpack. Who knows, if my life had been different maybe I would have stayed on longer – I was enjoying it so much. In two years' time, once he's finished college, my son Charlie has said that he'd really like to study at Manchester Metropolitan University. Maybe then I wouldn't be so torn if I were up in Leeds for weeks on end, I don't know. Charlie actually wants to study drama – can you believe it? All that education and I'm going to end up with another actor in the family. God help me!

Anyway, once *Emmerdale* was finally over with, after Christmas, the next big thing for me would be the *Birds of a Feather* tour – and I was getting butterflies in my stomach just thinking about it! The idea had been to do a stage version of the very popular comedy show that I starred in with Linda Robson and Lesley Joseph back in the 1990s, and it had come about when David Graham and Jan Hunt, who own the Comedy Theatre Company, approached Steve about co-producing a tour of the show. They'd acquired the rights to put on a stage version of *Birds*, having previously done tours of *Dinnerladies* and *Keeping Up Appearances*. I was certainly up for the idea. After all, the last year or so had seen such a huge change in my life and I'd been doing things I'd never done before. So I thought, why not do something else that you've never done before, Pauline? A tour! Plus I had a feeling that the time was right for it. I'd thought the time was right to end the TV show when we did, and now I thought the time was right for *Birds* to come back. People seem to have very fond memories of the show – there's a great deal of nostalgia for it. So once Linda and Lesley were on board we were off and running.

David then sat through all 101 episodes of the series to get some ideas together for a brand new script, which he said would be all ready by the time I finished filming *Emmerdale*. Rehearsals would start in February, and I was very excited about it, but, as I said, dreadfully nervous, too. Of course I was nervous: I've never done a tour, and I'd done hardly any theatre in the last twenty-five years either. Yes, I did panto at the Hackney Empire when Emily was little, but it was hardly something I was accustomed to. First and foremost, I am, and always have been, a television and film actress. I did perform in one play at the Royal Court actually, but I didn't have much of a clue what it was about. It was quite surreal and I didn't really understand a word of it, so I'm not entirely sure that that counts. It's funny, even when I did the pantomime (which was *Dick Whittington*) back in the early 90s, someone could have had a bath in the amount of rescue remedy I got through just to get me on stage every night. You're supposed to dab it lightly on your pulse points – well, I was drenched in the stuff!

Luckily, during the run of said panto, I had Linda Robson alongside to help get me through it. It was at the peak of *Birds of a Feather*'s success, so the two of us together in a pantomime would have been a pretty big draw, I guess. I was playing a character called Ratbag Lady, and my big number in the show was 'I'm too sexy for a rat'. I ask you! Linda, meanwhile, played the fairy godmother, but she was an extremely fat fairy, I have to say: heavily pregnant with her son Louis. She got to say the immortal line, 'Five miles to London and still no sign of Dick,' which, as you can probably imagine, prompted quite a few colourful remarks from some of the grown-ups in the audience, what with Linda clearly about to give birth. I enjoyed it, I suppose, but when push comes to shove I'd rather be at home at Christmas, or on holiday: not dousing myself in rescue remedy in a dressing room at the Hackney Empire!

One of my worst ever attacks of nerves came when I did the Michael Parkinson show during the 90s. I truly thought my legs were going to give out when I heard the theme music start up and I had to walk down those steps. When I did finally get down on to the set, sitting down next to comedian Brian Conley, who's a friend of mine, and actor Bob Hoskins, my nerves hadn't improved any. I locked my hands together, tight, and my mouth went so dry that I could barely speak. In fact, during a break in the recording, Brian had to lift a glass to my lips and feed me a sip of water because I was so petrified and I couldn't unclench my hands. It was Michael Parkinson, for God's sake! I remember saying to myself at the time: Don't do this again, Pauline, it's not pleasant; you're not enjoying the experience, so just don't! I suppose I've got a tiny bit better with television interviews over the past two or three years, simply because I've done more of them, but they're certainly not at the top of my wish list of things to do, and they never will be.

A few months ago I had to host five shows at Her Majesty's Theatre, and I was literally hyperventilating in the wings at every one. Luckily, once I get up on stage, something seems to take over and I'm generally OK, but the nerves never go away completely. The shows at Her Majesty's were to showcase the talents of the young people from the Pauline Quirke academies of performing arts, of which there are now thirty. Steve and I set up the first one in Beaconsfield in September 2007. There were a few reasons why we decided to do this: one of them was that I'd been acting for forty years, which truly was a milestone and I wanted to somehow mark it. Another reason was that I was becoming more and more aware and concerned about the cult of, and the obsession with, 'celebrity', which continues to be so prominent in the UK. It just seemed to me that so many young people were far too preoccupied with fame, and being famous, and which celebrity was doing what with whom, and all that malarkey.

Even though I was a child actor and worked professionally at a young age, the idea of celebrity concerns me: not only as an actress but as a parent, too. It's become a phenomenon, and it doesn't seem to be slowing down any. On top of that, the media seem to encourage all this avid curiosity about famous people and their lives, so I guess in some ways it's inevitable. I was horrified when I read a survey of under-sixteens who were asked what their ambitions and vocations in life were. Something like 85 per cent of them said that they wanted to be famous. Not an actor, or a singer, or a model . . . just 'famous'.

The idea behind the Pauline Quirke academies was to get back to the grass roots of how I started in the entertainment business. The little acting club I'd joined while I was still at primary school was very laid back and relaxed, and kids didn't join it because they wanted to be famous, they got involved because they wanted to act and have a bit of fun.

Now, God knows I'm no drama teacher, but I have got a fair amount of experience, and I wanted to pass some of that experience on. I wanted to be able to teach kids the basics of the performing arts in a responsible and truthful environment, and that's how PQA was born. We started it all off in our little office at home, with Steve and me just talking and talking about what we wanted to achieve, and then bouncing ideas off one another. We needed to come up with a game plan about what we could offer the kids who came to our academy, and then work out exactly how we were going to run it. I found it really gratifying to be working hands-on with Steve on a project together, because we were both really excited about it, and eager to get everything just right.

After much discussion, Steve and I decided on three separate modules, which would be split into one-hour classes: musical theatre, which combined all types of song and dance; drama and comedy; and for the third hour, film and television – which kids seemed to be fascinated with. The film and TV module would teach the kids how techniques varied from theatre to TV and then again to movies, and they learned to handle cameras, and also got to perform to camera. A typical academy day would run for three hours, with the children doing all of the three disciplines each time they attended, with their separate tutors.

When we started the first PQA, it was all very modest, with me filling out the children's application forms by hand, laminating their security passes and personally writing and sending them all birthday cards. Of course, now we have 1,300 children in the thirty different academies up and down the country, the birthday cards have fallen by the wayside, I'm afraid. The academies are based in schools, which are all checked out by our good selves, and take place at weekends, and each one has a different principal who runs it. The reason we use schools rather than, say, a village hall or community centre is because schools are designed with children's safety in mind, which is, of course, very important to us. Schools also have the right facilities: a good space for drama, a dance studio perhaps, so it makes much more sense. It's essentially a club, and the kids get to make friends outside of school, learning about responsibility towards others and working together as a group. I was really chuffed one Saturday when I spotted some of our Beaconsfield academy kids on the common, all having a picnic together on a day when the academy was closed. Children are exposed to so many different skill-sets when learning performing arts: they gain confidence, they learn to express themselves clearly and eloquently to other people, and they learn the skill of listening – a dying art if ever there was one. Most of the time our academy kids don't even realize these skills are coming to them because they're too busy having fun, but hopefully they are abilities that they'll carry into other parts of their lives.

Even Charlie went to our local academy before he joined the National Youth Theatre, and he loved it. He has now learned, partly from having a mum who's an actor and partly from meeting like-minded people at the National Youth Theatre, that there's a lot more to any kind of show business than just 'being famous'. There's a lot of work and dedication involved, or at least there should be! That's what Steve and I want to show the children at the academies, I suppose, as well as making sure they have a lot of fun into the bargain. In fact, the ethos of PQA is 'fun not fame: be yourself – be amazing!' There are some children who are better at singing, some better at dancing, some better at acting, but anyone can join and take it at their own pace. It doesn't matter if you're the so-called nerdy kid, or the cool kid, or the kid who never gets picked for anything at school. Drama doesn't differentiate. I'm very proud of what we've achieved, but we certainly couldn't do it without our incredible creative directors, Sarah Counsell and Simon James Green.

The shows at Her Majesty's Theatre were over five Sundays, and during that time every single academy got to showcase the theatre projects they'd been working on – on a proper West End stage. It was really exciting for them – and us too! The theme of the shows was 'American dream', and it was up to each individual academy to interpret that theme in their own way. Steve and all the wonderful people in our office organized the whole thing brilliantly, in conjunction with Her Majesty's, and I have to say it was fantastic. It really was of a West End standard. The tickets were sold to the kids' parents, friends and family, and any profits went to Children's Hospices UK. It was so amazing to watch those kids, some of whom I remembered being terrified on their first few visits to PQA, performing on a proper stage. There they were, on the stage at a West End theatre, giving it large, unlike the show's host – yours truly – who was shaking in the wings. Hopefully, by the time the *Birds of a Feather* tour started I'd feel a bit less jittery about it – but somehow I doubt it!

16
Back with the Birds

In preparation for the tour's promotion, a photoshoot was organized for Linda Robson, Lesley Joseph and me that I had been really looking forward to. The original 'birds' all back together again! A few weeks earlier, I'd been a bit worried about my old friend Linda. I'd called her, as I often did, and left messages for her and I'd sent her texts too – but I didn't hear a thing back. It was very unusual and I started to think all sorts of terrible things might have happened. Was she all right? Her mum had been poorly, was her mum all right? I'm sure I would have heard if something had happened, wouldn't I? Had I done something to upset her? I just couldn't fathom why she hadn't at least sent me a text. She hadn't even replied to my invitation to the vow renewal yet, and when I'd sent her a follow-up text asking if she could make it – still nothing! When my birthday rolled around on 8 July there was still no contact, and I knew that something was amiss. Linda always called or sent me a message on my birthday. What on earth was wrong?

The following day I was on *This Morning*, talking to the lovely Eamonn Holmes, whom I've known for years, about my weight loss and my recent traumatic storyline on *Emmerdale*. Little did I know that Eamonn and Ruth Langsford had lined up a couple of surprises for me into the bargain. After chatting to them about the ins and outs of my diet for a while and then looking at some clips of my performance as Hazel, Eamonn announced that there was an 'old actress' who wanted to pay tribute to me. Suddenly, up popped Lesley Joseph with a video message, telling me how wonderful I looked. It was so good to see her, and she didn't look too shoddy herself!

'She doesn't age,' I laughed to Eamonn. 'I don't know what she's on but she hasn't aged at all!'

That wasn't all, though. No sooner had Lesley signed off than on to the set came Linda, singing the *Birds of a Feather* theme tune. I had no idea she was even in the studio, and it had all been set up as a big surprise. Of course, off went the water cart! I was in tears the second I spotted her. I hadn't seen her for so long, well over a year; being away in Leeds so much had made it difficult to see much of any of my friends.

'You didn't answer my texts,' I blubbed at her as she came towards me. 'I was going to text you today to ask if you were OK because I was so worried.'

I was crying my eyes out on live TV, soppy cow, but I was genuinely so thrilled to see her. Linda then explained that she'd been too scared to speak to me, or even message me, in case she put her foot in it and spoiled the surprise that *This Morning* had so meticulously lined up for me.

'I knew I'd blurt it out,' she said, 'so I thought it best not to speak to you at all.'

Then she gave me a big hug and told me how fantastic she thought I looked, and made me laugh by telling me she'd been hiding in a cupboard all morning in case I caught sight of her. By that time, of course, I wasn't looking so good, with mascara smudged around my eyes and running all down my cheeks.

'They spent four hours trying to get me to look this good, and now you've mucked it up,' I told her.

To be honest, the producers were lucky I didn't swear when Linda appeared. Being surprised on live telly like that can cause words to pop out of one's mouth that one might otherwise have been a tad more selective about. And I truly was gobsmacked when she toddled on.

When the three of us did get together for the photoshoot in August, there was a lot of warmth and more than a few laughs. It was great to see Linda, as always, but now Lesley was there too, making it extra special. I'd actually not seen Lesley for two or three years, apart from the video message on *This Morning*, and I have to say she really did look brilliant. The photoshoot was mainly for the tour website, as the tickets were due to go on sale at any moment and people were already showing a keen interest. This made me even more nervous about the whole thing.

'It's all right for you two,' I said to the girls, who I knew both loved being on stage. 'You've both done loads of theatre, but I'm petrified!'

But as they well knew, I always *had* been nervous, even when we were taping the television episodes in front of a live audience, twenty-odd years ago.

It was hardly surprising, either. When we were recording the first series of *Birds*, before it had ever been televised, none of the audiences who turned up at the taping really knew what they were coming to see, so they could often be a tad quiet. On one occasion there was a large party of old-aged pensioners in the audience who had actually come to watch Les Dawson's TV show, which was being recorded in the studio next door. Unfortunately for them, Les's show was oversubscribed and there weren't enough seats, so these poor old dears were ushered into our studio to sit through a recording of something they'd never even heard of, namely *Birds of a Feather*!

Well, they were disappointed, to say the least, and very quiet throughout, which is not what you want when you're recording a comedy show really, is it? To top it all, the coach they'd come on was due to leave the BBC before we'd finished the recording, so, three-quarters of the way into the show, about 40 per cent of the studio audience simply got up and left the building!

I was always aware that even though *Birds* was a television show, we still had a live audience to satisfy as well, and that's where my nerves came in. Some of those people had driven a long way to watch us, and unlike the folks at home watching on the TV, they couldn't turn us off and watch something else. They had to sit there on hard seats and watch right to the end – unless, of course, they had a coach to catch before we'd finished. We all felt the same about it: entertaining the 8 or 9 million people who watched us across the country each week was important, yes, but it was just as important for us to put on a fantastic show for those 200 or so people in the studio.

As the photoshoot got under way we had more than a few good laughs. There was no stylist at the shoot, just us three old girls, who all turned up with a couple of different scarves each and what have you, plus our own clothes. We had a few shots done as ourselves: Lesley, Linda and Pauline, and then a few more in character: Dorien, Tracey and Sharon.

'Me and you don't look any different in or out of character,' Linda said to me.

It was true, there wasn't much difference; but I'd brought a denim jacket along for Sharon as she was always a bit more butch than the other two girls. It's funny, Sharon was also the fat one, and the butt of a lot of Dorien's comical jibes: but what now? Steve suggested, light-heartedly, that I might even have to wear a bit of padding on stage during the tour, just so we could keep some of those old 'fat' gags in.

Now that would be a turn-up for the books, wouldn't it?

17

The Clear-out

Back in the Dales, Hazel's life, unlike my own, wasn't getting any rosier, I can tell you. Her relationship with Aaron was at an all-time low because he blamed Hazel for encouraging him to end Jackson's life. In fact, he couldn't even bear to look at her. I know: it's confusing if you haven't seen it, so I'll keep it simple. Anyway, suddenly Aaron was threatening Hazel with a monkey wrench and bad-mouthing her, and it had all gone terribly wrong. On the upside, Hazel was offered a job in the café, and it's always nice to do a bit of 'café acting', because you get to work with and see so many of the cast as they pass through for a barm cake.

Skinny Minnie was my nickname at work now,

which is a moniker I wouldn't ever have imagined would be thrown my way. 'All right, Skinny Minnie? How are you?' Weird! I suppose the drastic change was more apparent to some of the cast and crew who weren't filming scenes and storylines with me every day. Sometimes you don't see one another for a few weeks at a time if you don't have any scenes together. Still, there wasn't one scrap of negativity from anyone on that set, and for that I was grateful, especially after some of the press stories I mentioned earlier. The other thing that pleased me was that the producers and scriptwriters of *Emmerdale* had made a conscious effort not to make a big song and dance about Hazel's weight loss. As I've said, it had been mentioned in passing when I'd started to shed the pounds back in the spring, but apart from that it was simply accepted as a gradual thing, and nobody harped on about it on the show.

There was another little bonus to being lighter that I hadn't really considered, and that was how much easier a day's filming was. I had to film a scene with Danny and me walking through *Emmerdale* village, which we rehearsed four or five times, and then did at least the same number of takes. Six months before I would have been knackered after just one stroll up and down that village – which is on a slope – and I certainly don't think I'd have been able to do it ten or twelve times. When I was playing Maisie Raine, who was a police detective, I would often have to jump out of a car, or run up a set of stairs to catch a baddie. That was before I'd had my hip replacement, and when you weigh as much as I did and you've got dodgy knees, that sort of thing can be excruciating – especially when you're doing it five or six times to get the shot just right.

'Can we start the shot when she's already out of the car?' I'd ask sheepishly after the fourth or fifth take. 'Can we start the shot from where she's reached the top of the stairs, please?'

Most of the time, of course, the directors were accommodating, but I still felt embarrassed having to ask.

There's also a lot of hanging around on set when you're doing any TV show, and during the filming of *Emmerdale* the old me would have had to sit down after a little while because it actually hurt when I stood for too long. One of the prop boys would usually be hovering at the edge of the set with a chair for me, and I'd be very grateful for it. I guess they could see I was in discomfort, poor old girl! Now, here I was marching up and down the village like a good 'un, and when one of the prop boys would ask me if I needed a chair, I'd say, 'No thanks, lad, you're all right!' Standing up was just fine.

Nevertheless, I was still terribly shocked when I saw photographs and watched film clips of myself before the diet. I just never thought I looked like that. Even when they'd shown some of my early *Emmerdale* appearances on *This Morning*, it had been a real jolt watching 'fat Pauline' up there on the screen. How could I have let myself get that big? Did I not see it go on? Well, no, I actually didn't! Seeing pictures of myself at the start of 2011 really brought home to me just how much I'd been kidding myself about so many things: the way I looked, my health. It was no wonder I needed a hip replacement with the amount of weight my hips were bearing. It was hard to connect the woman in those pictures with me any more. But it *was* me, and I could never let myself forget it.

So why hadn't I done this wonderful thing five years ago, or even ten years ago? I did have a real sense of regret about that, I don't mind admitting. Unfortunately, though, you can't tinker with the past, much as we all want to sometimes. I just had to accept that I was someone who needed a fair few kicks up the backside before springing into action, and that's the way I was made. Still, I resolved not

Above: In Majorca a few years ago for my fiftieth birthday with my lovely husband, Steve, who organizes the best surprises. I thought it would be a rather low-key break, but he only went and arranged for all our best friends to fly out and join us there!

Right: I might be smiling but Christmas 2010 was one of my lowest points. I was nearly 20 stone – nearly the weight of a sumo wrestler! – and in agony with my broken arm.

Above: Just after Steve and I got married in 1996, I was asked to do a holiday programme in India. So here I am, sharing my 'honeymoon' with the locals . . . and a camera crew!

Below: I've never been a fan of heights, so what could be better than allowing yourself to be driven up the Himalayas by a driver with a death wish? Stage fright may have plagued me throughout my career, but this was the only time I've ever had to take a sedative.

Above: Our son, Charlie, doing his mum and dad proud with a reading at our vow renewal in summer 2011.

Below: Following a swift costume change to a lovely purple number, with our good friends Max and Jo Clifford later that evening. Max and I are both vice-patrons of the Rhys Daniels Trust, and I don't think people realize what a lovely man of great integrity and honesty he is.

QUIRKE

Above: The Quirke clan on *All Star Family Fortunes*: (*left to right*) me, Steve, Steve's daughter Lauren, Emily and Charlie. Some might argue that we lost, but I prefer to say we came second.

Big hugs from Charlie, who has a heart of gold (*right*), and out at lunch with Charlie, Emily and Steve's nephew's little one (*below*).

Away from work, Steve and I – and Bailey, the dog – spend a lot of time on our boat *Vida Amorosa*. One tip, though: don't match your outfit to the upholstery, or vice versa. Not a good look.

I love what a good bra and a bit of slap can do for you! On the set of a LighterLife photo shoot just a few weeks into the weight-loss plan.

Four and a half months into the diet, I'd lost almost six stone and was feeling so pleased with myself. Wild horses couldn't drag me away from my first red-carpet outing of 2011 at the British Soap Awards in May (*left*). Later in the year at the TV Choice Awards (*below*) was a different story, though – I couldn't see a thing for all the flashbulbs going off and was more than happy to get out of there.

New York, New York! With two very obliging policemen, who must get this kind of thing from tourists all the time (*left*), and off the LighterLife packs and standing on my own two feet with a plate full of veggies (*below*).

It's been a roller-coaster year, but it would have been so much harder without my wonderful family.

to dwell on it, and to take advantage of the 'new me' as much as I possibly could. One of these advantages, and a complete revelation to me, was clothes shopping. Now I know us girls are supposed to love a good root around a dress shop more than we love our own children, but I've always been one of those sad people who get more joy out of buying a new duvet set for my bedroom. However, being a size 12 to 14 (the last time I was a size 14 was when I was about fourteen) opened up a whole new world of outfits, as I've already mentioned, so I found myself developing a real interest in clothes and fashion. A trifle late at fifty-two, you might say, but better late than never, eh?

With this in mind I decided that my wardrobe at home needed a bloody good clear-out, so one weekend in September I set about the task. I pulled everything out on to the floor, ready to sort it into piles of 'yes', 'no' and 'maybe', and off I went. Well, it was quite an eye-opener, I can tell you. As I said earlier, my idea of high fashion had been basically anything that didn't have a stain down it, and besides that, the bigger the better: anything to cover myself up. I surveyed the six huge piles of clothes on my bedroom floor, and boy were there some shockers in amongst them. It felt as if my whole life was laid out in front of me: years of panic buying and futile outings to dress shops for the larger lady. A bad-outfit graveyard!

The last time I'd seen a collection of clothes that dreadful was in a suitcase belonging to my own husband. Now Steve's taste in clothes is actually quite good these days, largely thanks to Emily and Charlie pointing him in the right direction, fashion-wise; but when we first got together it was absolutely grisly! I remember going on holiday to Mallorca with him, early on in our relationship, and being utterly horrified by the clothes he'd brought along. It was bad enough that he always matched the colour of his glasses to his shoes, but when that colour was often red, or sometimes yellow, it was even worse. Steve was a Club 18–30s holiday rep once upon a time in the 1970s, and I think you can pretty much get the picture from that. It was like Timmy Mallett on speed.

When we arrived at the hotel in Mallorca, I decided to unpack while Steve went in search of some extra pillows. It was then that I was faced with the suitcase from hell. Don't get me wrong, I was no fashionista back then, not by any stretch of the imagination, but there are some things in life that are just inherently wrong, and a fair few of them were staring up at me from that case. Now if some-one had been designing costumes for an amateur production of *The Wizard of Oz*, they'd have possibly killed for the contents of Steve's suitcase, but for me it all had to go – starting with the ruby slippers! When Steve eventually came back to the room, he was gobsmacked to discover his fairly new girlfriend gaily flicking the ash from her Benson & Hedges cigarette into one of his prized red-leather shoes – I felt it had more purpose as an ashtray, you see. The other red shoe I had tossed out of the hotel window, over the balcony, just in case poor Steve got any bright ideas about cleaning out my new ashtray and wearing it again.

Now here I was, years later, faced with my own breathtakingly appalling fashion blunders. I mean, how many black vest tops does a woman ever need? Really! What had I been thinking? There were also a fair few items that hadn't even had the labels removed, so either I'd never worn them or I'd been walking around, looking pretty silly, with a great big tag hanging off me. There were even some hideous, HIDEOUS monstrosities that I can only assume must have been bought in a moment of 'Oh my God! I must get something to wear for this, that or the other, so I'd better just grab something fast.' The question was, had I ultimately performed this task with my eyes shut? Surely I must have, I decided, when I found myself holding aloft a shocking number that I'd stumbled upon in amongst the heaps of clothes. I suppose one might describe the pattern on the fabric as 'floral' but I feel that would be misleading, not to mention overly generous. In fact, it looked rather more like something I'd been wearing whilst being violently sick all down myself, very shortly after eating tomato soup and chilli con carne. It was just horrendous! The only conclusion I could reach as to why the hell I'd ever bought the thing was that it must have fitted.

'Oh, that's a size 28: I'll take it!'

There were also an alarming number of lumberjack shirts (obviously from when I was going through some sort of Canadian Mountie phase) which I'd almost certainly grabbed off the rail simply because they fitted at the time. They had to go as well, as did the wealth of three-quarter-length trousers in varying shades of black: black cotton with an elastic waist for the summer, black nylon with an elastic waist for the winter. Everything had to have an elastic waist, and almost everything had to be black.

I'd never been a great one for buying loads of shoes, and being the size I was before, I just wore what was comfortable. There was one particular pair of flat pumps with straps across that my kids hated with a passion, and I can't say I was surprised, really.

'Mum, you look like a fool, those shoes are horrible!' Emily, never one to mince her words, would say.

I think she and Charlie would have happily set fire to them, they were so ugly, but they were comfortable and, at the time, that had been my one and only criterion. Now I was looking forward to wearing a bit of a heel if I went out somewhere nice, which I'd never have considered before (unless I'd wanted to be in agony seconds after leaving the house), and tights, and skirts – it was all possible now.

After uncovering a few more stinkers I decided I wasn't going to throw the clothes away but take them to a charity shop (although I'm not entirely sure what sort of person would want some of them, apart from the odd lumberjack). I made a decision that I would not, under any circumstances, keep hold of any of my bigger-sized clothes – 'just in case I grew back into them'. I'd done exactly that the first time I did LighterLife: when I hadn't taken the counselling seriously, or explored the route to management part of the plan. I did a similar sort of wardrobe exorcism then, but I hung on to quite a few of my bigger-sized clothes, even though they didn't fit me any more. Now I wondered if, subconsciously, I'd known that it wasn't the right time back then. Maybe I'd already convinced myself that I didn't have the willpower to stick at it, and that I'd ultimately fail. As it turned out, I had been right in that sad assumption.

This time it was all going: the comedy fat-suit dresses, the 2 million oversized black vest tops – all of it! It all had to go. And it was not like I'd been buying loads of new gear, either. I'd decided not to go rushing off on mad shopping sprees. For a start, I hadn't settled yet, weight-wise, and what was the point of buying a pair of trousers that were going to be too big a month after I'd bought them? The other reason was that I was still discovering what kind of things I actually liked to wear. It was something that hadn't really crossed my mind before, and why would it? As I said, if it fitted and it was clean, I wore it! I was still finding my feet as far as fashion went, and there was no reason to rush. I wasn't going to put the weight back on again this time.

I had now got five pairs of jeans though, and that was a real novelty – I was living in the damn things. I'd not been able to wear jeans for years before the diet. I'd also bought a couple of dresses towards the end of the summer, and, of course, my gym stuff. I still don't think that anyone over thirty should wear leggings outside in front of the general public, so I skulk about in those behind closed doors. Apart from that, I would just have to wait until I reached my target before I punished the credit card too much more, and even then I wouldn't go mad. I struggle to justify, for instance, spending a fortune on one single item of clothing. I spotted a beautiful leather jacket one day when I was out looking for a suit for Charlie to wear for college, but the jacket was £150. That, to me, is a lot. I know some folk wouldn't think so, but I do. I mean, for me to spend that amount on a jacket it would have to do the housework for me, and make me a cup of tea when I asked it to. It would have to be some special leather jacket! I also decided to keep my beautiful suede jacket: you know, the one that I adored but was too small for me one minute and too big the next? I didn't keep it because I thought I was going to grow back into it one day, I kept it because it symbolized something for me. It was like an icon of my weight loss and it always will be; and now it was sitting in a much emptier wardrobe – for the time being, at least.

18

Boat Porn

One of the other big changes that Steve and I have come to accept in the past year or so is that as our children are getting older they no longer want to spend all their holidays with us. It's a bit sad for me, but I suppose it's the way things have to go. At the time of writing, Emily is twenty-six and Charlie sixteen, and the last thing either of them want to do is to stare at us pair lying around on holiday when they could be off doing something much more exciting with their mates. Since we sold our villa in Mallorca two years ago we've tended to stay in hotels whenever we're there, and, as I said, it's not something Charlie was interested in doing any more, unless he was able to bring one of his mates along. So enjoy your holidays with your children when they're young, I say, because it's not going to be that way for ever.

With this in mind, Steve and I started thinking about . . . boats! Now we'd been on a couple of boating holidays: we did France when the kids were younger, and a few other places, too. And from these trips I'd learned, without question, that I was absolutely useless at opening and shutting locks, mooring, or in fact anything that required any degree of coordination as far as boating or sailing was concerned. I knew my place – in the galley making the tea – and that was how I liked it. Despite all this, I found boating holidays a lot of fun – we all did – so when Steve and I realized we were becoming ever more fascinated with TV shows about barges, it was definitely food for thought. Living by the canal in Leeds, too, I'd found myself looking out at the barges with wonder, and so one weekend Steve and I decided to rent one for ourselves.

We picked up the barge in Skipton, then travelled along the Leeds and Liverpool Canal, having a great time along the way. Don't get me wrong, it was hard work, and on this trip none of the locks we went through were manned. When there's only two of you and the barge is 70ft long, it's definitely all hands on deck whether you like it or not. So when we came to a lock, Steve would stay on the boat and navigate it in, and yours truly (hyperventilating all the way) would get off and open and close the lock, containing my nervous hysteria as best I could. As I said, it was hard graft, but to me, working together as a team made it all the more fun. It was just me, Steve and the dog, and I think that's the way our holidays will be going from here on in. Luckily, Steve and I like one another enough for that to be just fine, although there were a few sticky moments when I had to endure him barking orders at me. Not good!

'PORTSIDE! AFT! STARBOARD!' he'd be yelling.

'What? What? Just say left or right, for Christ's sake!'

It's a real test of a relationship being out on the water together, I can tell you, and one thing I learned about myself on that holiday was that I'm not at my best when instructions are shouted at me. Somehow, Steve and I always managed to get through the day without any actual blood on our hands, and we'd laugh about it later in the evening.

So that was how we whetted our appetites for 'a life on the ocean wave', so to speak, and pretty soon we'd taken things one step further: something we christened 'boat porn'! Yes, on evenings when I was at home, Steve and I would toddle off to bed armed with magazines like *Canal Boat*, which was filled (as you may have already guessed) with articles about barges, boats and waterways galore.

As time went on, though, we moved away from the notion of a barge and started to think more along the lines of a cruiser. Not a 'gin palace' boat – we weren't setting our sights on a vessel resembling Khashoggi's yacht: just a nice, smart cabin cruiser. Mind you, I also knew that I didn't want a boat so small you had to convert the dining table into one of the beds of a night, like some of the old-fashioned caravans I stayed in as a kid. Nor did I want to stumble over sleeping bodies every time I wanted to get to the galley to put the kettle on in the morning. If we were going to get a boat, I wanted a boat with two separate bedrooms and a little bit of space, so we knew what we were looking for. The thing was, we couldn't find it anywhere! So, like most things in life, we just thought, It'll wait, and we put the idea to one side.

Then while we were away on holiday in Mallorca in August, a boat-broker friend of ours emailed us photos of a boat that had just come on the market that very day. It was lovely! But it was also in Holland. So, just a day and a half after we got back from Mallorca, we flew out to Holland to view it, and the day after that the boat was loaded on to a trailer to be transported to England and to us! Two days later it was back in the water again – in the Thames, right near our home. It was absolutely beautiful: a 32ft, two-cabin, steel-hulled cruiser, which, once Steve had all the relevant licences, we'd be able to take out to sea if we so desired. We loved it!

The funny thing is, it was on a boating holiday that I'd actually met Steve – when I was about twelve. It was many years later that we ended up as a couple, but that holiday was the first time I ever clapped eyes on him. My aunt and uncle took me to the Norfolk Broads as a treat and they were friends with Steve's mum and dad, who lived near them in the Balls Pond Road area. Steve was fourteen at the time, and I guess we became mates simply because we found ourselves on holiday together. A Norfolk Broads holiday back then basically involved the grown-ups sailing from pub to pub, so us kids would end up sitting in front of a riverside drinking establishment with a glass of R. White's Lemonade and a bag of Golden Wonder crisps. I thought he was a nice enough lad, but I was much too young to get moony-eyed over boys back then, so being mates was only ever as far as it went. I didn't see him again until I was nineteen, when he'd sometimes come in to have a drink at the pub where I worked, and the next thing I heard was that he was living in Mallorca. Ours was certainly not what you'd call a whirlwind romance! Still, that boating holiday in the early 1970s must have made some kind of impression on the pair of us, as we've both developed such a love of being on the water.

We'd had to think of a name for our lovely new boat before we brought it back from Holland. It did have one already, which, roughly translated from Dutch, was *Farmer's Girl*, but we wanted to choose a new name for this marvellous vessel to make it our own. Much deliberation ensued (you have to get these things just right, don't you?) and there were many, many suggestions from the kids before we went to collect it – most of which were obscene. Charlie, for instance, suggested *Cock on the Water*, but we decided against that, for obvious reasons, and thought we might go for something with a Spanish flavour because of our mutual love for the country.

'Love life' is a phrase we thought was rather nice, which in Spanish is '*vida amorosa*' . . . or is it? After we'd had our chosen name emblazoned across our new boat over in Holland, we spoke to a friend of ours who lives in Mallorca, who told us that the correct translation of '*vida amorosa*' wasn't 'love life' as in 'to love life', it was 'love-life' as in 'how's your love-life, mate?' Oh well! We liked it, and that's what mattered.

For the next few weeks we grabbed every opportunity we could to get on board. The kids loved it, and I even started to meet my friends for lunch on it, rather than at home. I suppose I'm looking on it as something that Steve and I can enjoy for years to come: pootling along at our own pace, and getting to know this new and rather agreeable life on the water, where an hour feels like a day and a day feels like a week. The thing is, you have to take it so slow when you're on the water – three or four miles an hour – that you can't help but relax, really; but it's not like I'm lying around for hours on end, drinking cocktails and flicking through a copy of *Hello!* magazine. There's always something to do, whether it's tying the boat up, opening and closing the locks or making the tea! That's all part of it for me, though, and I've grown to love it.

I even went for my boat-handling test, for which I hoped to receive a certificate declaring me water-worthy. The test entailed a day out on the water with an examiner – on my own, without any help from Steve. I felt like it was important because I was still a little intimidated by the boat, to be honest, and I thought that knowing a bit more about it would help me overcome that fear. So, on a gloriously beautiful day, off I went.

Now the good thing about this particular test was that you don't have to memorize a whole load of stuff before you take it, not like a driving test. It's all about the things you learn on the day, which was quite a relief to me, to be honest, as I didn't have a stellar record as far as any sort of vehicle-related examinations went. I failed my driving test three times before I finally passed at thirty. The first time I tried, aged seventeen, ended in a minor disaster when I sort of . . . shall we say, nudged . . . a woman who was crossing the road in front of the car I was driving. Now I have to say in my defence that she wasn't on a crossing of any description, in fact she stepped off a traffic island right as I was passing. Of course, when I saw her, I slowed down to let her cross, even though I, technically, had right of way. However, I perhaps misjudged my braking distance slightly, and/or miscalculated her position in relation to the car and . . . well, as I say, I nudged her. I didn't knock her to the ground or up in the air or anything, but I certainly gave her a bit of a fright. FAIL! It probably didn't help that I was so nervous during the test that my right leg began to tremble severely (something that often happens to me when I'm anxious) – not good when one's foot is on an accelerator. Even before the nudging incident, the examiner had made me pull over to the side of the road to calm down for a minute or two before resuming.

It was my crippling 'stage fright' about this sort of thing that made me fail my driving test again when I took it a year later. It was only when I was working on *Birds* twelve years later that I even thought about attempting a test again. There were quite a few exterior shots of Sharon and Tracey pulling up outside the house in a car during the series, and neither Linda nor I could drive. We would take the handbrake off while two props men pushed the car along so it looked like we were driving. Eventually someone on the production team suggested that it might be useful if Linda and I took our driving tests. Even then it was Linda, who wasn't fussed either way, who passed, while I failed and had to take it *yet again*, finally succeeding on my fourth try. The funny thing is, I've loved driving ever since and am

pleased to report there have been no further inci-
dences of 'nudging'!

With the boating test, first and foremost, I had to
familiarize myself with the workings of our particular boat. Now I know nothing about the finer
points of boat engines, and I hope I'll never have to,
but I had to at least know where the main things
were and what they all did. I also learned how to
throw a rope properly when in a lock, tie a few
different knots, and about steering, mooring, safety
procedures, wind direction – you name it! Then I
had to learn about manoeuvring the boat into the
correct position in case I had to rescue someone
who had fallen overboard. My particular charge in
this exercise was a blue bucket called Bob, who was
thrown overboard for me to save over and over
again. After the third or fourth time I lost all
patience and told the examiner that if Bob threw
himself in the water again he could bloody well stay
there. Anyway, at the end of the day I passed and
I've got my certificate to prove it. The next exam is
the helmsman's exam, which I will no doubt take in
due course, when I'm feeling like another challenge.

There was one more thing that the arrival of *Vida
Amorosa* prompted too, and that was a spurt of
shopping! Steve and I rushed out and bought

everything with a 'nautical' look we could lay our hands on. Blue and white paper cups and plates, duvet covers, whatever! It was really great to get excited about something together, and I couldn't wait for our first holiday on the boat, even if it was just me, Steve and Bailey the dog from now on.

19

Hitting the Target

My goal, as far as weight loss went, had always been to get down to 11 stone, but at the end of September that unexpectedly changed. (What's this? I hear you cry.) I was cruising along nicely at about 11 stone 8, and one day I went shopping for a pair of trousers. Grabbing a size 14 off the hanger, I tried them on, only to discover that they were too big for me.

'I'd say you were nearer a size 12 now,' the woman in the shop said, smiling.

'Am I?'

I was a little surprised, to be honest, and while I thought that being a size 12 was rather wonderful, I actually felt like I didn't want, or need, to lose very much more weight. I suddenly felt right exactly as I was. OK, so what now? Was it time for me to take the next step? Was it time for me to go on to the route to management stage of the plan? Yes, I decided, it was. Of course this was going to mean making choices: making my own decisions about what I put into my body. Yes, I know I'd had a short period of experimentation when I was in Mallorca, but this was the big one. I was going to be eating proper food again every single day on top of my three LighterLife packs. There was a whole world of potential stumbling blocks and temptations before me, but I knew it was time. It's funny, because all the time I'd been losing weight I had this magical target of 11 stone in my head, but at the end of the day my body told me when I was at the right weight. I just sort of knew it!

It wasn't so much what I saw in the mirror – because that had been so gradual, and over such a long period that I don't think it ever really hit home. It was more of a general feeling. To be honest, the diet had never been about looking better anyway, that was just part and parcel; it was more about improving my quality of life. Now my clothes looked and felt right (but funnily enough it was taking me so much longer to get dressed because I had so much more to choose from) – I felt comfortable and, for the first time in three and a half years, I felt like taking Bailey for a walk. Although when I picked up his lead the poor animal just looked at me, confused, as if to say, 'You? No, you don't do walking, love!'

And while I was strolling round the beautiful area where I live on a sunny autumn day, stopping at the village café that I'd never stopped at before because I'd never walked that far, I thought: Yeah. I'm all right now. I'm just right.

So did I go out to a posh restaurant with Steve to celebrate reaching my ideal weight and my return to proper food? I did not! I decided that celebrating would have been making a big deal of it, and therefore making a big deal out of the food I was going to eat: as if it were some longed-for prize at the end of a gruelling task . . . a treat! That was the kind of thinking I neither needed nor wanted. Having one proper meal a day, and making the choice about what that meal consisted of, was merely the next step in my plan for a new attitude towards eating, and I decided to view it as such. This is just how it is now, I told myself.

Happily, what I did want to eat was fish. I discovered tilapia fillets on the fish counter at

Waitrose, and for those first few weeks of proper dinners I couldn't get enough of them. They're a freshwater fish and not much to look at (you certainly couldn't describe them as the George Clooney of the fish world) but I love 'em! I'd have one or two fillets with a bit of salad or some vegetables, and I was quite happy to eat them almost every night.

I was also finding that on the occasions when Steve and I did go out to a restaurant, I was more than content to go for the less fattening choices. I was actually drawn to them, in fact – phew! For instance, when the two of us went to one of my favourite Italian restaurants in Leeds, San Carlo, I had a vegetable platter to start, and then headed straight for chicken with a tomato sauce and some salad. I wouldn't have dreamed of raiding the bread-basket, or tucking into a bowl of tiramisu. I had no desire for either, and I was very pleased I didn't. Maybe it was down to all the counselling I'd done, but I now saw a sausage roll for what it was: flour, fat and water, mushed together and then rolled around a trail of fatty meat. I deconstructed the food that I'd enjoyed so much before, but which I knew was bad for me. Cheese, for instance, which I still love the taste of and could certainly have from time to time, I now saw as a block of yellow fat. It wasn't that the taste wouldn't have been nice, but I knew it for what it was now. Not a reward, not a treat, but a tasty bit of yellow fat! In fact I didn't even care if I never had another potato on my plate again: it just meant less peeling! Despite all that, I *did* still have to stop at all the same pesky service stations, and I *did* still smell the sausage rolls, and they *still* looked and smelled appealing. Just not appealing enough for me to eat, that's all.

The other new thing for me was that I stopped taking milk in my tea and I started eating fruit. Before I embarked on LighterLife I'd never have dreamed of having fruit as a snack, but suddenly a satsuma was just the ticket. Of course, I still had my trusty packs to hand, which made things easier for me, especially if I was eating on the run. Having the packs tucked away in my bag meant that there was no reason for me to have to grab a shop-bought sandwich, for instance. I just had to make sure I could get to somewhere where there was a kettle, that's all.

The idea from now on was to ease yourself into completely normal eating over a period of time. As the packs go down, the normal meals go up. My plan was to try to be eating proper food full time by

Christmas, and at the start of October that didn't seem that far away. You can't drive yourself mad with it, though! I was having one little pot of low-fat yoghurt each day for a bit of extra protein – and yes, I knew it had sugars in but it was a yoghurt, for God's sake! If I started obsessing about every little thing I'd just become boring. I'd seen other people do it and it wasn't me.

I can still bake a chocolate cheesecake without sampling it, so I need to give myself a bit of credit where credit's due, don't you reckon? You've got to think about how you feel and what you want, and if that means having a glass of wine every now and again, then so be it. Ultimately, I wanted to make this new world of healthier eating a natural part of my everyday existence, not something that dominated and dictated the rest of my life. Where's the joy in that? Any horrendous downfall I encountered would simply be due to old habits, and as I've explained my particular old habits were pretty full-on. The boredom eating, the eating in advance of being hungry: I hoped I'd learned to combat all of that behaviour, and would continue to do so.

The mainstay of my support during this period of adjustment, apart from Steve and my kids, were the counselling sessions that I still took part in. By this time, a lot of the other ladies that I'd started off with were now on the route to management phase of the programme, so it was nice chatting to other people who were in the same boat. 'Celebrate what you've lost – but don't celebrate it too much!' And that's the way I felt about it, I guess. I didn't want this anxiety about what I ate hanging over me for the rest of my life. In the future I'd dearly love to be able to say: 'Yes, Pauline Quirke, you may have a sliver of cake if and when the occasion arises, and no, you don't have to beat yourself with a birch twig afterwards, or look shamefaced about it on the high street for the next two weeks.'

My simple little plan was to get on the scales every week, keep an eye on my weight, be aware of how my clothes felt on me (by that I mean keeping a check on whether my jeans were feeling a bit more snug than they had the previous week) and just moderate my intake without letting it take over my life.

That said, we'd already planned a family holiday in New York for Christmas and the New Year. New York? Christmas? The two things together might sound like a recipe for dietary disaster to most people, and they'd probably be spot on. Yes, I'd most definitely have to be on full alert there, but at the end of the day I'd got to trust myself, hadn't I? The only person who could muck up was me, and that was all there was to it!

20

A Greek Tragedy

By the end of September Linda, Lesley and I got the first draft of the *Birds of a Feather* theatre script, and we also had a big day of *Birds* TV and radio promotion lined up for the start of October. The tour had begun to feel very real, as had my imminent departure from *Emmerdale*! In fact I was now so acutely aware of how little time I had left working on the show that it made me very sad every time I thought about it. That very week I'd popped into the scheduling office to see if they had any idea when my last day of shooting might be, just so I could give the designated organizers of my leaving do (Lucy, Danny and Charley) a definite date for the party. One minute I was calmly asking Ruth, the girl in the office, when she thought I'd be finished for good, and the next I was suddenly crying. Yes, the water cart was off and rolling! I was really not looking forward to saying goodbye to these people, I can tell you. They'd become wonderful friends, and I was going to miss them.

On the upside there was a big *Emmerdale* party that weekend to look forward to. It was a fantastic way for the cast and crew to let their hair down and, as it turned out, the perfect opportunity for yet another post-party fiasco for yours truly. (Remember the valet parking debacle after the soap awards?) Anyway, this do happens every year at a hotel not far from the studio, and I decided to take a friend of mine, Sue Broadfoot, who lives in Brighton and is a huge fan of the show. During the day we went round the purpose-built village where *Emmerdale* is filmed, then, once at the party, we relaxed and had a couple of glasses of wine (which I hadn't been able to do at any of the previous *Emmerdale* gatherings post-Christmas 2010) and we had a bit of a dance, a bit of a giggle and a really good night!

The following morning, which was a Saturday, I was filming at the studio, and when I got back to the flat in Leeds I couldn't find my phone. Had I left it at the studio that morning? Damn! So all the way back to the studio I went – but no phone!

'I've only gone and lost my mobile,' I whined to Steve from the flat. 'I definitely had it at the party. I know I did, because I called a cab with it, so I've either dropped it in the cab, or at the hotel after I phoned.'

So we called the cab office controller, who got in touch with the driver who had taken us home from the party. No phone in the cab. OK, so I must have dropped it at the hotel, and no, I wasn't tipsy! Bugger!

So I jumped into my car and headed for the hotel, hoping that some kind person might have handed in my missing mobile at the front desk. I jumped out of the car and trotted up to the hotel entrance, which was quite narrow, and found myself heading into a large group of people, all swathed in black clothing and looking rather sombre. They'd clearly just been to a big funeral, and from what I could gather they were mostly Greek. Now, what I probably should have done was stand back and allow them all to pile into the building, and just wait until the way was clear to pass through into the lobby. For some reason, I decided to jump right into the midst of the throng, wriggle through, and head straight up to the reception desk to see if they had my precious phone. What a mistake. Within seconds I found myself jammed in amongst what had swiftly become a fast-moving line of mourners, all dressed in black, with me in the middle in my jeans and a gleaming white T-shirt. I simply couldn't escape, and was being carried along with the grieving mass towards an important-looking man just a few feet away. It was then that the penny dropped and I realized that in all likelihood he was the head of this huge family, and we were filing past to respectfully shake his hand – and I was now in the bloody queue!

I tried to move backwards, but it was impossible as more and more people continued to pass through the door – it was like trying to swim upstream. I tried to shift myself sideways, but there just wasn't anywhere to go, so I put my head down and kept going with the crowd: straight towards my un-avoidable meet and greet! It was obvious that a fair few people within the multitude had clocked this strange and apparently griefless woman, flailing around manically and trying to shove her way through the crowd, and I was getting my share of funny looks. What could I do? What would I say?

'Hi, my name's Pauline and I'm having a bit of a nightmare!'

Quite suddenly, a gap miraculously appeared before me as I reached the front of the queue – like the parting of the Red Sea – and I speedily darted to one side, running towards the reception desk and away from the crowd. God knows what those poor people must have thought.

'Who the hell is that mad mourner in the jeans and white T-shirt?' is my guess. How embarrassing.

To top it all, the people at the reception desk were rather unhelpful, and my phone wasn't there either. It definitely hadn't been handed in.

'Well, can I go to the room where we were last night?' I asked the receptionist, still flustered. 'You never know, it might be there, near where I was sitting.'

It was a long shot but worth a try, I thought. When I reached the room I pulled open the door with a flourish, and yes, lo and behold, there was the entire Greek funeral party, all sitting there, waiting for their post-funeral sit-down dinner. Great! So here she is again, the mad woman in the white T-shirt, the funeral stalker: and look at her, crawling around the floor in the corner looking for something that isn't there. One last cursory glance around the room, and I skedaddled as quickly as I could. *Sans* phone.

And do you know what? The following Monday when I got to the studio, there was my white phone sitting on actress Sammy Winward's white phone charger, precisely where I'd left it on the Saturday morning!

The following week, all three birds – Lesley, Linda and myself – did a whole day of press and TV to promote the tour, and also to herald the release of the complete *Birds of a Feather* DVD box set. We did a really fun slot on *The Alan Titchmarsh Show*, where they played several clips of *Birds* and the three of us reminisced about our time working together and how much we used to laugh during filming. And boy did we laugh! Doing *Birds* really had been like ten years of going to work with my best mate . . . and then laughing all day. Every morning during the filming of the series Linda and I would take our children off to school, then we'd meet up to be collected by a car that would drive us to the studio for 10 am. We'd rehearse until 2 pm and then be back in the car ready to pick our kids up from school. Of course, we had lots of work to do on our scripts after that: line learning and suchlike, but that would all be done when we'd fed and bathed the kids and tucked them up in bed. It's actually quite tough to think of one particular incident that makes me chuckle more than another when I think about the ten years I spent on *Birds*, but few days passed without somebody saying or doing something silly that would leave us in hoots of laughter.

When it came to the recording of the show, however, we were always very speedy. We'd usually rehearse from Monday to Thursday, and then on the Thursday night we'd record the show in front of the studio audience at 7.30. If we weren't all up in the bar by half past nine then something had gone terribly wrong; in fact, our little post-show drinks became pretty legendary at the BBC. Working with more or less the same cast and crew for ten years, we became like a big family, and each week everyone would bring a few guests up to the bar, turning what should have been a quiet after-work drink into a party that went on and on. After a while the people who ran the bar at Teddington Studios got so pissed off trying to get us to leave at closing time, they'd just hand us the keys and tell us to lock up on our way out. Then, one night, one of the lovely electricians on the crew decided that what our parties really needed was a karaoke machine, and so one was duly installed in the bar.

Now of course Linda and I thought we were

marvellous singers, especially after a couple of glasses of vino, but we weren't exactly modern in our choice of songs to perform, even back then. We'd do 'You Made Me Love You', 'Ma, He's Making Eyes At Me' and 'What Do You Wanna Make Those Eyes At Me For?': barely making it into the 1920s, repertoire-wise, but they were certainly our favourite numbers. After all the nervous tension I built up before a show, these parties – plus a good sing-song – were a great way to let off steam and wind down. And the best thing about it was that we all got driven home – it was perfect! That being said, Linda and I would still have to be up to take our kids to school on the Friday morning, hangover or not, but on the whole we had a fantastic time. I really don't know where those ten years went, and now here we were, ready to do it all over again.

21
Coverage

During October there seemed to be a tremendous amount of press coverage about me and my weight loss, and not all of it positive. Sure, I'd done a few hand-picked interviews on the subject, but those interviews would then be syndicated, and on top of that, one or two publications just made it up as they went along.

'People must be thinking, Bloody hell, not her again!' I said to Steve.

My face seemed to be everywhere and it was getting to the point where even I was fed up with looking at me. The bad press was hurtful, too. I tried not to let it affect me, not to even read it, but it's hard to look away once you've seen a headline screaming out your name from a supermarket shelf. One day on a front cover I'd spotted a very unflattering picture of me coming out of the soap awards. I was looking slightly shocked and bemused – as you might well do when you have fifty-odd cameras going off in your face all at once – and it was one of those special 'up the nose hole' camera angles, which are never that great at the best of times. The headline was *Desperate Pauline turns to a stranger for help*. Really? It was too tempting not to read, although in my heart I knew that it was going to upset me.

It turned out that the mysterious 'stranger' was in fact my LighterLife counsellor who I talk to every Monday night during our group sessions, just like everyone else on the plan. Hardly a stranger after nine months, but there you go. Luckily, I didn't buy the magazine; I just stood in the Co-op and read it, but reading something negative about yourself when you're trying to be positive is hurtful, and I'd be lying if I said it didn't bother me.

I tried to keep hold of the massive sense of achievement I felt, but with that sense of achievement came a terrible anxiety that I just couldn't shake. It was an anxiety that crept up on me, a feeling of panic that I eventually had to voice to Steve because it was preying on my mind all the time.

'I feel like I'm carrying a huge weight on my shoulders because of all this coverage I've had with the diet,' I told him after yet another story appeared. 'It's such a big responsibility and it scares me.'

The negative comments hadn't helped, I suppose, but for some reason I was suddenly overwhelmed by this newly inherited burden, and I felt like I had a responsibility not only to LighterLife but also to anyone who might have been inspired by my diet, to all the friends who had been so tremendously encouraging, and to the *Emmerdale* fans. I even felt like I had a responsibility to the people who think I'm going to get fat again – a responsibility to prove them all wrong! It seriously started to get to me. And while 99 out of 100 people heaped words of praise and encouragement upon me, I would focus on the one bad comment I'd heard on any particular day. I guess that's human nature! I just had to keep telling myself that I must shake it off, and that's what I tried to do. I'm a real glass-half-full person at the end of the day, and I intended to keep it that way. It wasn't going to be easy, though. That much I did know.

There was one piece of press that I did like. In fact, I was thrilled to bits when I read it. Tony Parsons, who writes for the *Daily Mirror*, and whom I've never met, wrote a truly lovely snippet in his column about how inspiring to women he thought I was, and how brilliant it was to see someone losing weight without a surgical procedure.

'What a beautiful woman, what a fantastic role model,' he wrote. 'No gastric bands, no surgery, just willpower and a vigorous diet. Pauline is leaving *Emmerdale* and looks like she's ready to take on Hollywood, and start dating Warren Beatty!'

Apparently, he was comparing me to Annette Bening, Warren's wife, and there was a shot of them next to the one of me to show the comparison. The funny thing was that one of the directors on *Emmerdale*, Pip, had told me that I looked like Ms Bening quite a while back, but I hadn't taken too much notice to be honest. Still, there you go! I'm not sure how thrilled Annette would be with the comparison but I was chuffed to bits. Tony's lovely piece really was a shot in the arm during a difficult time, and it's now stuck to the front of my fridge for posterity.

All this press coverage also raised the question in my mind of whether my weight loss might have an impact on the type of acting parts I was offered, but I guess I'll have to wait and see about that, won't I? As I've said before, I've never taken on the role of someone who was defined purely by her size, and how I've portrayed a particular character has never been affected by how big I was. I mean, when I played a grieving mother in *Our Boy* I wasn't running around shouting, 'Oh God, my son's dead and I'm a size 18.' It had no relevance to the part. Suddenly, though, my appearance had changed quite radically. It wasn't just about being thinner either; now people were seeing me looking a bit more glamorous, with a posh frock and some slap on. Maybe it *will* throw a new perspective on me as an actress and the sorts of parts I'm offered. Mind you, I doubt if some things will ever change: I'll always get cast as the maid rather than the lady of the house, but that's got more to do with my accent than my weight! It will be interesting, though, to see if anything does come my way that might not have previously. A gangster's moll, perhaps?

One thing that definitely has affected my job as an actress more and more recently is my deafness, which has got steadily worse over the years. I'm now completely deaf in my left ear, and I've lost about 30 per cent of the hearing in my right. I knew it was getting bad a few years back when Steve and I had to move everything around in our bedroom because I couldn't hear the TV.

'Can you turn it up a bit, Steve?' I'd be asking constantly, but Steve would be moaning because it was really loud.

The thing was, to face the TV I would have to lie with my good ear on the pillow, so I could hardly hear a thing. So, eventually, the TV had to be shifted to the other side of the room. It was at that point that I paid a visit to an ear specialist, who informed me, after tests, that I'd lost 60 per cent in my left ear but that my right was fine. Since then, however, the hearing in my left ear has deteriorated to nothing and my right ear has got worse.

'It's like trying to run a marathon with one trainer on, Pauline,' a specialist in Huddersfield told me last year. 'Your right ear has been overworking to make up for the fact that the left one doesn't work at all; and because of that the right one is now getting worse.'

Apparently I suffer from a build-up of calcium in the bone inside my ear, no one knows why, and that's what's blocking my hearing. The specialist said that I would need to start wearing a hearing aid, and these days, he informed me, they were fantastic and virtually undetectable. He was right; the hearing aid was fitted exactly to the shape of my ear and was indeed very tiny. The only problem was that once I was wearing it, everything was suddenly super-loud! I'd been so used to living with such a small amount of natural hearing that the shock of being able to hear so well suddenly was just too much for me.

I had to have the hearing aid tweaked once, and then again, so that the world wasn't quite so loud, but while I was wearing it on the set of *Emmerdale* I still felt like I could hear every tiny little sound. One morning a crow flew over my head. Well, I honestly thought that the Luftwaffe were about to drop bombs on the village, it was that loud. Every crunch on every piece of gravel sounded like an avalanche, and while ordinary hearing people would naturally filter out many of the background sounds, my hearing aid just seemed to amplify everything and I couldn't get used to it. One day on the set of *Emmerdale* I was in the middle of filming a quiet scene with Danny in the village, when I suddenly heard a woman talking at the same time as I was. I glanced around but couldn't see anyone, then realized that the soundman, who was holding a huge microphone and wearing headphones, could hear the voice as well. Nobody else seemed to be able to.

'Where *is* that woman's voice coming from?' I asked him.

'How on earth can you hear that?' he replied with a look of surprise. 'It's someone talking in one of the houses and I'm picking it up on the mic.'

The person talking was well out of normal earshot, but of course with my bionic hearing aid I could hear her clearly and it was more than a little off-putting having someone else talking over me while I recited my lines. Sadly, in the end, the noise was so terribly distracting that I had to stop wearing my hearing aid altogether.

I know that with perseverance I'll probably get used to the deafness, and I suppose, ultimately, that's what I'll have to do, but what with getting used to the diet and then a whole new way of eating I felt like it was all too much at once: one thing at a time, Pauline, one thing at a time.

The downside of this mini-defeat was that I continued to encounter little problems on the *Emmerdale* set as well as off it. I sometimes missed what people had said and had to ask them to repeat themselves, and I'd often miss cues as well as lines. It wasn't so much the volume of people's voices I had difficulty with, it seemed to be a tonal thing. Whatever it was, there were times when I completely missed the word 'action', which is not great when you're an actor.

I guess my ears are just another little part of me that's getting decrepit as I grow older. At least, unlike my hip replacement and my broken arm, it was nothing to do with my weight. I mean: they're not weight-bearing ears, are they?

22

Knees Up

I was noticing that I now had a zest for wanting to get out and do stuff that I certainly hadn't felt for a long time before, and I had all this extra energy going spare. It was hard to recall a time when I'd felt as well as I did in the gorgeous, sunny October of 2011. I suppose it should have been obvious, really. After all, I wasn't shovelling loads of unhealthy foods down my throat every five minutes, and I was exercising regularly: I guess it's not rocket science, as they say. I also felt, despite the recent anxiety I'd suffered, that I was thriving mentally as well as physically – like I'd achieved something wonderful and faced so many demons in the past few months, and I'd come out the other end victorious.

It was a nice feeling: like I'd just run a marathon, and I wanted to enjoy it – without being too complacent, of course!

However, I wasn't out of the woods completely on the health front, and I was about to feel a little bit more of the fallout from weighing almost 20 stone not that long ago. If I'd ever needed a reminder of why it had been so vitally important for me to shed all that fat, here it suddenly and unexpectedly was.

A month or so before, I'd had some aches and pains in my knees, but I'd put that down to the fact that I was going to the gym regularly and using the treadmill. Perhaps, I thought, my poor old knees were simply getting used to all this new activity, or maybe I hadn't been warming up and stretching enough before I exercised. Anyway, it wasn't too serious so I just sort of carried on regardless. Then one day at the studio, I was walking along the corridor, on my way to get a coffee from the canteen with Lucy, when I suddenly had the sensation that my leg had been kicked out from under me. I have to say it was quite scary, and painful too.

'Oh my God, Pauline, what just happened?' Lucy asked, as I steadied myself.

'I've got no idea,' I said, slightly flabbergasted.

'My left knee just completely went, as if it couldn't support me.'

Later that week it happened again, and then the next couple of weeks there were a few more incidents. Pretty soon it had gone from happening twice a week to twice a day and it was always the left knee: something was definitely wrong. So off I hobbled to a doctor in Leeds, who duly referred me to a knee specialist, also in Leeds, who, we were happily informed, was the best in the country.

It was clear from the X-rays that something wasn't right. One of my knees looked completely different from the other. It turned out that apart from having osteoarthritis, which is what I'd had in my hip, I also had a piece of bone sticking out of the side of my knee, which was jarring somehow and making my leg give way. In fact, my left knee wasn't sitting in its correct position at all. Now whether that displacement was a result of my fall the previous Christmas I didn't know, but I did know that just like my hip, my knees had been carrying around a lot of extra weight for a very long time. The upshot was, I was going to need surgery, which meant I was going to be laid up at home and off work. Not good! I'd only just gone back to *Emmerdale* after a long break so the producers wouldn't be too pleased about me being out of action again so soon. Fortunately, I'd already booked the half-term holiday off, so I could have the operation in that week. My recuperation would need to be quite speedy, to say the least!

The operation was set for a Friday, and on the Thursday evening I was doing a night shoot for *Emmerdale*, which involved Hazel finding a baby in a telephone box and then running through the village back to her house to try to save its life. Of course, it wasn't a real baby, it was a very realistic little jelly one, but the running was certainly real, and there was lots of it! Mercifully that night my leg held out, despite being very painful; and all the time I was aware that any minute I might go over, which certainly wouldn't have been any fun – for me or the little jelly baby!

After the operation I was just in hospital for the night and then Steve took me back home in the car. I have to say, three and a half hours in a car after a knee op is not the most fun I've ever had, but luckily I was still full of drugs so it was bearable. Then it was a week's rest in Buckinghamshire, though most of that week was spent trying to remove all the arrows that the surgeon had scribbled on my leg! As it turned out, I was fighting a losing battle, as he'd clearly drawn all over me with a permanent marker! What with that and Steve having to put a surgical stocking on me every morning and take it off every night, I can't say I was feeling my most glamorous. Still, at least it was done.

I was a bit gutted, though. I'd originally booked the half-term holiday off so I could spend time with Charlie and perhaps go out on the boat with Steve, but now here I was hobbling around at home, unable to do very much at all. I'd discovered all this new energy and sense of well-being, but I couldn't do any exercise at all, even get out on my new bike. How frustrating! The upside was that now, at 11 stone 7, I would certainly get over it all a damned sight quicker than I would have when I was eight stone heavier. I'd realized that even when I left the hospital and got into the car with relative ease. I mean, how much healing time would I have needed if I'd had the operation a year before? A lot more, I reckon, don't you?

I suppose it was quite fortunate, to be honest, as I had to be back at work within a week whether I was better or not. Still, at least the writers and producers at *Emmerdale* knew what was going on with my knee, so I wasn't anticipating any major stunts for Hazel once I got back on set: no jumping off roofs or rolling through the village, thank you!

By the time I did get back on the *Emmerdale* set, we were filming stuff for the Christmas period. One morning I had to film a raging argument with Lucy, which was a whole lot of fun. I must say it's a weird way to start your day, having a big screaming match with one of your closest friends, but there you go. It was particularly odd because behind the scenes that day we'd been busy organizing a girly weekend in the Lake District with some of the other *Emmerdale* girls. I was then filming a scene for the Christmas Day episode, where Hazel is walking through the village and it begins to snow. As snow was in short supply at the end of November it obviously wasn't real: our snow was actually foam pumped out of a big blower. Still, it looked very real and very pretty nonetheless, and it was just magical walking through the village as the snow fell all around me. The *Emmerdale* set would never look as beautiful for me as it did that day.

One Monday morning, after a lovely couple of days off at home in Buckinghamshire, the phone rang as I was about to do the school run with Charlie. The call was from one of the assistant directors on *Emmerdale*, a guy called Peter.

'Good morning, Pauline,' he said.

'Hello, Peter,' I chirped, 'and what can I do for you?'

'Where are you at the minute?' he asked.

'I'm at home, Peter, why?'

'Leeds home?'

'No, Buckinghamshire home.'

'Oh.'

An ominous silence followed.

'You're supposed to be on set, Pauline; you have scenes this morning. Everyone's waiting for you.'

I felt the colour drain from my face instantly. For some unknown reason I hadn't put the two scenes in my schedule and therefore had completely forgotten about them. On most occasions when I had scenes after a weekend off, I'd get a phone call from someone like Peter to remind me, but that hadn't happened either. Had I been in Leeds, of course, I could have been in a cab and at the studio within the hour, but getting there from Bucks, which is 200 miles away, was a whole different ball game. The repercussions of this are huge on a show that runs a schedule as tightly constructed as *Emmerdale*'s. They couldn't write me out of the scenes because they were linked to other, upcoming plotlines and scenes, which would then also have to be rewritten. Having an actor go AWOL with no warning really does cause a major headache for the production team.

You know those recurring nightmares some people have? The ones where you regularly dream about something you've always dreaded actually happening? Well, that's always been mine. I've always dreamed about not being where I should be. Trying to get to the place I'm supposed to be, but not being able to. Letting everyone down! In fact I've actually had dreams where I'm sitting in my kitchen having a cup of tea before receiving a phone call asking: 'Where are you? Why are you not here?' And here it was, actually happening. I felt awful, but thankfully the *Emmerdale* production team is pretty good at juggling schedules at a moment's notice, so I didn't get into too much hot water.

After three weeks back at work I was getting rather impatient with my knee. It seemed to be taking a long time to heal, and I was still in a lot of pain. It felt sort of 'crunchy' to me, so I went to see the consultant, who reassured me that three weeks was not enough time for it to have healed completely, particularly as I'd been walking on it. I guess I just wanted to get back to normal as soon as possible. The whole incident was like one little final reminder of the damage I'd done to myself being as heavy as I was, and now I just wanted to put all that behind me and move on. I was thoroughly enjoying feeling healthy for the first time in years.

23

Saying Goodbye

For the last weekend in November I arranged a special treat for three of my best friends from the cast of *Emmerdale* and my daughter Emily: a girly weekend of relaxation and pampering at a gorgeous hotel in the Lake District. Very posh! I'd got on very well with pretty much everyone during my time on the show, but these girls – Lucy Pargeter, Charley Webb and Zoe Henry – had become very special to me, and I wanted to do something to show them just that. I suppose it was a thank-you for making me feel so welcome when I'd joined *Emmerdale* and for being so wonderfully supportive during my diet, as much as anything, and although there was a big leaving party in the offing in a couple of weeks' time, I thought it would be rather nice if we girls did something fun together before that. All three of them have young children and don't get that many opportunities to sneak away with their mates for a weekend, so we were all really looking forward to it.

We were due to set off from Leeds for the two-and-a-half-hour drive as soon as we'd all finished shooting on the Friday, and we were hoping to get away sometime in the early afternoon. As it turned out, Nada, the man who is head of scheduling on *Emmerdale*, kindly swapped a few bits and pieces around which meant that none of us had any scenes to do that day after all. So there we all were, standing in the Yorkshire TV studio car park first thing on the Friday morning, swigging bucks fizz and toasting our weekend away – well, apart from me and Lucy, who couldn't drink because we were both driving, so were stuck with an orange juice and no fizz!

It was good old Yorkshire weather that day, so not great, but not too bad either, and while I was driving Emily and Charley, Lucy took Zoe in her car. Well, true to form, we'd scarcely got out of the car park before I got lost – after approximately thirty seconds, Lucy turned right and I turned left.

'Lucy's gone the wrong way,' I said smugly.

After all, my trustworthy sat-nav lady had told me to turn left, and whatever my sat-nav lady tells me to do, I bloody well do, no matter what!

After a minute or so, off went my mobile phone, and sure enough, it was Zoe asking why the hell we were going in completely the opposite direction from where we were supposed to be headed. That'll teach me.

When we did eventually arrive at the hotel, which was the Old England Hotel and Spa, right on gorgeous Lake Windermere, we weren't disappointed. Emily and I had a lovely room that overlooked the lake itself, and the staff at the hotel couldn't seem to do enough for us. There were already chocolates and champagne in our rooms (always a nice touch!) and I'd also made little gift bags for the girls, which included socks, scented candles and nice bath stuff, to open as soon as we got there. What a very nice start to the weekend! As well as the gift bags, I'd bought each of the girls a bangle with a little heart on, and in return they'd given me the most beautiful antique link-bracelet, which completely bowled me over.

From then on we proceeded to spoil ourselves rotten. We went for some great meals, squeezed in a shopping excursion, had some spa treatments (I wasn't keen on having hot stones stuck on me, thank you very much, and I'm allergic to some of the products used in facials, so I plumped for a nice massage), and the rest of the time we just spent chatting and laughing and enjoying one another's company. It was perfect! When we went for dinner at the hotel restaurant on the Saturday evening, the hotel management organized a cosy private lounge for us so we could gossip away to our hearts' content without being disturbed or worrying that someone might be watching us or listening in to our conversations. It's not as though anything we were saying was particularly salacious or even that interesting to anyone else, but the fact is that we were four ladies from a TV show on a night out together, so there was a chance that we might attract a bit of attention. Yes, we may have just been talking rubbish, but it was our own private rubbish!

To finish off a perfect weekend, we all decided that we fancied eating fish and chips in the car while looking out over the lake. The fact that we couldn't get the car near enough to the lake to actually see it, or that it was teeming with rain, didn't deter us! As we sat there, tucking into our fish and chips, it dawned on me that a few months earlier I wouldn't have been able to do so. I'd have had to sit there eating one of my snack bars, just savouring the smell of the vinegar fumes, but now I felt I could join in. This made me think about just how much my attitude had changed since I'd lost all the weight – I now knew that I *could* trust myself to eat some of the foods I thought I'd never be able to eat again without craving them the next day or the one after that. I guess that's what the counselling had done for me. It had made something as simple as sitting in the car in the pouring rain, eating freshly fried fish and chips, a precious moment. Not because I thought of the fish and chips as a treat or a reward, but because, finally, I could trust myself to choose what I ate.

Back on set the following Monday afternoon, we bored everyone stupid at the studio telling them how terrific the weekend had been. But it really had been a fantastic way for me to say thank you and farewell (for the time being, at least) to my lovely new mates.

The following weekend was my official leaving party, which had been organized by Danny Miller at a swanky club in Leeds called The Loft. The invitations and posters around the studio heralded the event as 'Pauline's Well Posh Do' with a dress code of 'as posh as you like', and sported a picture of yours truly pulling a pint behind the bar of the Woolpack Inn. Sad though I was to be saying good-bye to everyone en masse, I was really looking forward to the party itself.

Of course, with it being another big party night, surely there had to be one more Pauline Quirke calamity, just like the valet parking and Greek funeral debacles that had gone before. I have to tell you, folks, I didn't disappoint! On the day of the party, I noticed that a handbag I'd recently bought in Debenhams was broken slightly – one of the little buckles had come loose and fallen off. As Emily and I were going shopping in Leeds that day, we decided to pop back and see if the store had a replacement. I'd used the bag a couple of times, but as it was practically new the lady behind the counter was happy for me to take a new bag in exchange for the broken one, and off we went on our merry way.

Later that night, I was getting all dolled up for the party – putting on the lovely black sequined party dress and fabulous black suede shoes I'd just bought – and I thought, Ooh yes, I must remember to wear the gorgeous antique bracelet the girls bought me! I couldn't wear it all the time because it had to come off for filming – I mean, there was no way Hazel

Rhodes would have had a bracelet like that, so it came off along with my wedding and engagement rings while I was shooting scenes. Now where did I put it when I last took it off? Drawer? No. Bedside table? No. When did I last . . . ? Oh no! It suddenly dawned on me that the last time I'd worn my beautiful bracelet I'd also been carrying the handbag with the broken buckle. The one that I'd just returned to Debenhams in Leeds.

Wait a minute, though. I'd cleared the bag out before I'd taken it back, hadn't I? I distinctly remembered taking all the stuff out of the old bag and putting it into the new one. But had I cleared it out completely? Or maybe I'd just dropped the bracelet. Whatever had become of it, I felt terrible.

'Emily, I think I've done something really stupid,' I confessed.

By this time it was ten past seven on Saturday night, but Emily went to the computer, found the number for Debenhams head office (thank God for Google!) and rang them straight away. They put us through to the Leeds branch, but of course the store was closed until Sunday morning by that time. There was nothing I could do.

It was a bit of a downer really, not only because I had to go to the party without my lovely bracelet and hope to God the girls didn't notice, but also because I couldn't be 100 per cent sure that the bracelet was definitely in the bag. And if it was, what if the bag had been chucked away because it was broken? It wasn't as if I could simply have replaced the bracelet with an identical one either – it was a flamin' antique! Anyway, it was no use worrying, so I tried to put it out of my mind and headed to the party with Emily.

As I walked through the door of The Loft I was faced with two life-sized cardboard cut-outs of myself: one very fat Pauline, and another that was super slim and glamorous! Poor Lucy, whose idea it was, had been in two minds whether to put them up or not.

'I didn't want you to be offended,' she said, but of course I wasn't put out in the least.

If anything it was a bit scary coming up against a life-sized likeness of my former, larger self, but it was a good laugh too, and I actually think those cardboard cut-outs got just as many dances, kisses and cuddles as I did during the evening. There were certainly plenty of photos taken with various party guests jammed in between the two Paulines with silly grins. They were looking a bit ragged and torn by the end of the evening, I can tell you.

I was genuinely delighted by how many of the cast and, in particular, the crew turned out for the party, and the night itself was truly momentous! We started at about 8.30 pm, but I said I didn't want any loud music until about 10 so that everyone would have time to mingle and chat without having to bellow over Beyoncé at full pelt. Once the music did start, however, I was up on the floor strutting my stuff for the rest of the night (though not, I have to say, in my gorgeous new suede shoes, which I'd only worn for approximately four-and-a-half minutes as they were absolutely killing me). I didn't have it in me to make a big speech as I'd felt very sad that whole weekend and really didn't want to get too emotional, but I did say a few short words to a sea of beaming faces:

'I've had the most wonderful time. I really have thoroughly enjoyed myself, and I've loved being on the show. Thank you all very much.'

Yes, short and sweet, but that was about as much as I could manage without too much blubbing!

After that, I was given the most perfect of parting gifts from everyone who worked on the show: a two-day course at Rick Stein's seafood cookery school in Padstow. And as if that wasn't enough, Lucy had made me two incredible photograph albums with pictures from my time at *Emmerdale*, on-set and off, plus magazine covers I'd featured on (fat and thin) over the year, and pictures of all the cast and crew with handwritten messages from each of them. It must have taken her absolutely ages to put them together and been a huge amount of work. Some of the messages made me laugh and cry all at once: Jeff Hordley, who plays Cain Dingle and is married to Zoe Henry, wrote: 'Gutted Cain and Hazel never got it on!' Danny Miller wrote: 'Thank you, Pauline; you've been like a mother to me.' It was fantastic, and I was absolutely over the moon with the whole evening.

Before I went home, the *Emmerdale* boss, Stuart Blackburn, asked me if I might like to go back for a guest slot in October 2012, for the show's fortieth anniversary. How could I refuse? What I loved about *Emmerdale* was that while the actors and cast members did come and go, the important thing was the show itself. It was nobody's vehicle: no one actor was more important than anyone else, and there was no star of the show either. I told Stuart that I'd love to go back if I possibly could.

By the time Emily and I left the party it was around 1 am, but apparently some of the diehards partied on until much, much later.

* * *

Of course, the very next morning I found myself standing in Leeds town centre in the cold, nervously waiting for Debenhams to open. When I eventually got to the handbag department, the staff there had already got the message that I was coming and why. Mercifully, the bag *was* still there, and after rooting around inside it I found my gorgeous antique bracelet. God, I was relieved. I'd put it in a zipped side pocket . . . to keep it safe, obviously!

24

One Final Curtsy

Towards the end of the year I travelled from Leeds to Manchester to do a TV commercial for LighterLife. I always think commercials are quite weird things to do because talking to a camera rather than to another actor feels a bit peculiar, and it had also been a long time since I'd been in one. Back in the 1990s, Linda and I did a series of TV ads for Surf washing powder. It was only four or five days' work at a time, but we did them for a few years running. I guess because those ads were just little sketches involving Linda and me playing competitive neighbours, they didn't feel all that alien to do, but the LighterLife one was to be just me – on my own – talking into a camera about a product.

Even the way they shoot commercials is different from anything I've been used to on a drama, and, as usual, I was terribly nervous. Still, at least I wasn't going to be waffling on about something I didn't totally believe in; I wholeheartedly supported LighterLife.

Anyway, the set-up of the advert was me, looking fairly glamorous in a turquoise top and black trousers, sitting in my fairly glamorous dressing room, complete with a star on the door, flowers, and chic furniture in tasteful muted shades.

'Sometimes, girls, dieting can get you down,' I say earnestly, before breaking into a grin. 'So my advice is to lighten up, with LighterLife Lite!'

Then away I go, explaining all about the system and the packs, showing off my new figure and finishing with a smile.

The first time it was shown on TV I got a text straight away from Lucy Pargeter, saying, 'Just seen you on telly, Mrs,' followed by the little routine she always does when she's impersonating me. She adopts a ridiculously heavy cockney accent, and sounds slightly mad:

'I 'AVE A PACK IN THA MOORNIN', I 'AVE A PACK IN THE AFTERNOON, AN' THEN I 'AVE ANUVA PACK IN THA NIGH-TIME!'

It's cruel but bloody funny.

Anyway, I think the advert came out all right in the end. I did try not to be too cheesy and actually said to the director on the day, 'The last thing I want is to come across as cheesy and smug.' So I'm hopeful that it looks OK and does the job!

By that time, as far as food went, I was eating almost normally again (not the old Pauline 'Greggs pasty' version of normal, of course, but what was to be normal for me from here on in). I did still enjoy a LighterLife porridge in the morning, and I'd still have the occasional pack at other times, but I was generally managing my diet properly without having a regime to stick to. Even with all the parties around Christmas time I'd managed to enjoy myself without going silly. Yes, I did have a few glasses of wine at the *Emmerdale* Christmas do, I just didn't have the customary kebab on the way home!

With this in mind, I'd decided that it was time to bid farewell to my LighterLife counselling group. I was about to leave *Emmerdale*, I was leaving Leeds, and it just seemed like the right time to stand on my own two feet. So at a meeting in December I said my goodbyes to the girls in my group, along with another happy lady who had also reached her target weight. I can't say that it had been plain sailing all the way – it hadn't. There had been times when I'd felt extremely vulnerable during my LighterLife diet, particularly when people who didn't even know me seemed to be having a pop at me – that was tough! And I'm not naive enough to think there might not be difficult patches in the future, either; but it's not as if I can't ever speak to Jo (my counsellor) again if I need her – she would always be there for me on the end of a phone. However, as far as the group went, that was that. I'd learned what I needed, and now it was time to put that knowledge to good use.

In December I also popped over to Derby to see my old mate Linda, who was doing panto with Paul Nicholas. The production was *Dick Whittington* and Linda was reprising her role as Fairy Bow Bells, a feisty, straight-talking fairy godmother – with a cockney accent, of course! It was wonderful catching up with Linda's mum and sister, and her nephews and nieces, as I hadn't seen them for such a long while, and after the show we all went out for dinner together – all twenty-two of us! Linda and I sat together and caught up with one another's news, or at least as much as you can when there are twenty-two people round a table, but she was excited about our upcoming *Birds of a Feather* tour, and I knew we would have plenty of time to catch up properly once that started. It was great to see her whole family together, but it's funny, I always feel a little bit sad whenever I see Linda's mum. I think it's because seeing her makes me think of my mum, who is no longer with me, and the good times we had when we were all so much younger.

Before I knew it, it was time to film my final scenes for *Emmerdale*. I'd already shot my last actual 'on screen' moment, but I still had a few scenes left to shoot that were to be screened before that. My last actual appearance on the show was with my dear mate Danny Miller, and I have to say it got quite emotional. The scene takes place in the village graveyard beside Hazel's son Jackson's grave, with Hazel and Aaron, who have had a roller coaster of a relationship, to say the least, saying goodbye to one another. Aaron and Hazel herself have both come to the conclusion that Hazel will have to move away from the village if Aaron is to have any real chance of moving on with his life. It was a real tear-jerker, and in the last moments of the scene the two characters are supposed to go in for a hug but then find they can't do it. Danny and I, however, disagreed with that one point, so we discussed it on the morning of the shoot and decided that the two characters should hug. Aaron had never been overly affectionate towards Hazel, but we felt that given how overwrought and emotional they both were, it just seemed right. So we hugged and we cried, and afterwards neither of us was sure whether it was Hazel and Aaron who were sobbing their hearts out, or Pauline and Danny. We were really going to miss one another.

Funnily enough, the last scene that I actually filmed, on Thursday 15 December, was Hazel's leaving do in the Woolpack. Now I'm not sure if the shooting schedule was worked out especially so that this was my final piece of filming (though knowing the *Emmerdale* team, I strongly suspect it was), but it meant a lot to me that it worked out that way. Hazel's goodbye in the pub was absolutely lovely! Lucy was there, as were many of my other mates in the cast, and Hazel says her farewells to all of them. We did a couple of rehearsals, and then two or three takes. Then suddenly the director said 'Cut,' and then I heard someone shout 'Clear!', which meant they were happy with the scene. My time on *Emmerdale* had come to an end. As per usual, the water cart was off and running and I got very teary, as did some of my friends in the cast. Then, as if by magic, crew members who weren't even working on the scene that day appeared on the set to say good-bye to me. Stuart Blackburn then presented me with some flowers and made the most beautiful speech. It's hard for me to remember all of it, given the emotional state I was in, but there are a couple of things he said that I'll never forget.

'When I first heard that Pauline Quirke was join-ing the cast of *Emmerdale*, I thought, Oh yes, that's the funny one from *Birds of a Feather*! But having worked with you, I now know that you are so much more than that. Apart from being a truly talented actress, you're also one of the nicest people I've ever worked with.'

As I looked around the pub set I could see the faces of all the crew, and all of my friends, plus other cast members who had been working on other scenes in other studios that day but who had turned up to see me off, and suddenly they were all applauding. I was completely overwhelmed. After all my forty-odd years' experience as an actress, to be made to feel that loved and appreciated by your fellow cast and crew is something very special. There was simply nothing I could say that could express how I was feeling. So I took one final little curtsy, and walked out of the studio.

I guess, if nothing else, that's one thing I've learned over the years. Always know when to keep your mouth shut!

It's amazing how much stuff one can accumulate in eighteen months, as I discovered when the time came to furiously cram all the bits and bobs from my Leeds flat into boxes, ready for Steve to collect me. I spent Friday packing and cleaning, and cleaning and packing, and when Steve arrived on the Saturday to load up the car I was ready to say ta-ta to Yorkshire for the foreseeable future. We didn't go straight back to London, however. At one of the *Emmerdale* parties I'd won a raffle prize of bed and breakfast for two at a luxury country house hotel called Wood Hall in Wetherby, West Yorkshire. I was quite pleased about this, as I'd only ever won a giant Easter egg from my mum's corner shop before, and that was when I was eight years old – and it turned out to be dark chocolate, which I hated and wouldn't eat. So a night in a luxury hotel was a bit of a result, to be honest, and Steve and I had a lovely evening together.

* * *

When we finally reached good old Beaconsfield on the Sunday, I was very glad to be home, and as I began to get used to the idea of being back for good, I thought about what a double-edged sword the whole *Emmerdale* experience had been. When I thought back to December of the previous year, I realized that I couldn't have been any lower. I was ridiculously overweight, my diet had failed, I was unhealthy, and I'd just broken my arm so I was in constant agony. Add to that the fact that I was away from my home and my family and you have a recipe for a very unhappy Pauline. However much I had enjoyed working on the show, it still wasn't home, and when I'm feeling low that's where I really need to be.

But then, on the other side of the coin, being away from home and getting on with my job forced me to face up to my weight and health problems and do something about them. Having that goal, that dream, in which people would see me lose weight on screen week by week, as well as being surrounded by such wonderfully encouraging people at work, really helped me turn my life around.

Eventually I got used to being away from home, and the travelling became second nature to both

Steve and me. It worked out! It didn't stop me from missing my family, no, but I got through it. It was a huge learning curve for me as an actress and as a person, and although being away from the place where I'm happiest for eighteen months was bloody hard . . . I did it!

25

A Bite of the Apple

I was only home for two days before I was off again! This time, however, I wasn't leaving Steve, Emily and Charlie behind. We were going on a very special and (I think) well-deserved Christmas holiday – to New York! We were all really looking forward to it, but Charlie, who was the only one of us who had never been, was beside himself.

As we left for the airport, I may not have been overweight but my suitcase certainly was – it weighed a ton – and the reason was that, for the first time in many years, I'd packed more or less everything. I actually had lots of clothes that I wanted to wear: choice, I think they call it! In previous times I'd have had a Samsonite half full of black elasticated trousers, and a few black tops with enough extra fabric to make a quilt. Not now, though: I was going to hit the Big Apple looking super trendy – well, as super trendy as I was ever likely to get, but looking good, nonetheless. I hadn't bought any new gear especially for the trip, but after a year of dieting I'd gradually accumulated a whole new wardrobe. Luckily, neither of the kids took much as they intended to go shopping and buy lots while they were there, so I was able to sneak some of my overflow into their cases on the way there. It's funny, because I actually don't find the shopping that brilliant in Manhattan. I don't think anywhere is as good as England, to be honest.

The journey both ways was pretty pain-free; in fact, on the way back British Airways upgraded us to business class, which was a real treat. Not that Steve waited to be asked anyway, blagging us all into the BA business lounge before we'd even been given the upgrade – I don't know how he does it! Charlie doesn't fly very well, so he really didn't enjoy that part of the trip, but as soon as we got into one of the yellow taxis outside the airport, I could tell he was excited. Even the fact that we had a bit of a crazy driver added to the fun of the journey for him. And our hotel in New York, which was right in the heart of the city, was lovely but unassuming.

Manhattan is one of those places that you think you know, even if you've never been before. We've all seen the iconic imagery and landscape of the city so many times – in movies, TV programmes and countless cop shows over the years – and you really can't help but get swept up by the buzz of it. The constant noise, the yellow cabs whizzing by, the skyscrapers that just seem so unfeasibly high – it's all there, and all strangely familiar. Standing in Times Square itself, surrounded by all the screens and electronic billboards a mile high, is quite something, especially if, like my Charlie, you're a seventeen-year-old boy who's grown up in a little town in Buckinghamshire and has never been anywhere like it. I think he was a little bit overwhelmed with it all, to be honest.

Now those of you who have been to Manhattan will know that there are two things you can do a hell of a lot of while you're on holiday there: walking and eating! I was once again made acutely aware of what a huge difference my weight loss was having on my life, after trooping around seeing the sights and shopping for a couple of days. I just couldn't have done it before, I really couldn't: not at 19 stone 6, no way! The fact that my energy levels were so much higher now made this a completely different New York from the one I'd experienced in the past.

As for the food (which is everywhere you look in New York, and we're not talking small portions, either) – well, I ate what I wanted when I wanted it, I suppose . . . within reason! I mean, I never had one of those infamous American breakfasts: pancakes, maple syrup, bacon and all that malarkey. I couldn't eat like that now if you paid me – in fact, even the 'old me' wouldn't have eaten that kind of grub. No, I'd have fruit and yoghurt or a poached egg for breakfast – nice and sensible! For the rest of the time I was a bit more relaxed but still aware of what I was putting in my mouth. I certainly didn't start eating everything in sight just because I was on holiday, but I ate a few things that I wouldn't have had at home. I had a burger, for instance – just one, but that's something I'd normally avoid. Consequently, I put on a few pounds, but when that happened I realized that my attitude to gaining a bit of weight had changed, too. Instead of stressing about it, or going to the other extreme and thinking, Oh well, I've already put on a few pounds so a few more won't hurt, I just decided to be extra careful when I got home and get back to the weight I was before. After all, I'd lost eight stone, so a few pounds shouldn't be a problem. What I never want to get into the habit of is pigging out for a week and then going back on to LighterLife total to get it all off again. That's not the way it's supposed to work!

Anyway, as for the walking, there was plenty of that – I walked my legs off. We did all the usual sights: the Rockefeller Center and its Christmas tree, the Staten Island ferry past the Statue of Liberty – you name it! Plus I had the kids dragging me around the shops most days, so I was knackered by the evening and we were all in bed by ten most nights. Steve summed it up one day when he said, 'I've walked so much today, it's not my legs that hurt, it's my hips that are killing me.'

One evening, we took the kids to a New York comedy club, which they absolutely loved, and on Christmas Eve Emily and I went to see The Rockettes at the gorgeous Radio City Music Hall. The Rockettes are a very old-fashioned, all-singing, all-dancing group with plenty of high kicks, glitz and glamour. I suppose the nearest thing we had to it in the UK was the Tiller Girls, who I remember dancing at the London Palladium in the 1960s. Just seeing the Radio City building in all its art deco glory was fabulous in itself. On another day we took Charlie to Grand Central Station for the same reason – it is such a beautiful building.

I'd been to New York a couple of times before. I took Emily for her twenty-first birthday, and she loved it then. I had planned to take her for her eighteenth, but it wasn't that long after 9/11 and I was still a bit apprehensive. Even now I can't bring myself to visit Ground Zero – I think it would upset me too much. As it is, every time I see a New York firefighter I can't help wondering how many pals or colleagues he might have lost that day. It's always there in the air.

The other time I went to New York was when Steve took me on a surprise trip one year. He had bought me a posh handbag for my birthday – I think it was my thirty-eighth – which was a little strange because I wasn't particularly a posh handbag sort of a girl, so to speak. But when I opened the handbag, I found two tickets to New York, which was really exciting as back then I'd never been. Well, I had all sorts of romantic notions about being in Manhattan with Steve, and one of the things I'd dreamily pictured was the two of us riding through Central Park in a horse and carriage, eating a hot dog (yes, you knew there had to be food involved somewhere along the line!). Anyway, when we were there, off we went to Central Park, where we found a man to take us round the park in his horse and carriage, and Steve bought me a hot dog. Well, folks, that's about as far as I got with my Mills and Boon dream sequence. The hot dog was revolting, for a start! Then as soon as the carriage driver heard our accent and found out where we were from, he completely spoiled the trip by waffling on about how he'd married an Irish girl and how it hadn't worked out, and how she'd gone back to Ireland, and how heart-broken he was, and how much he loved her and missed her, and all the things he might do to win her back . . . and on, and on! I felt like saying, 'Enough! I don't want to hear any more about your bloody broken marriage – this is my moment!' It was too late, though, the moment was pretty much ruined.

Needless to say, we didn't bother with a ride round the park on this trip.

Our Christmas Day in New York was unusual, to say the least, but it was exactly what we wanted – something different! We'd all agreed that we wouldn't give one another big presents, so the plan was to buy gifts up to the value of $10 and no more. I got a scented candle, amongst other things – I do love a scented candle – and I bought some sweets and a few little bits and pieces for the kids to fill up their

Christmas stockings. The only thing was, silly Mum had forgotten to bring their Christmas stockings, so I had to rush out to the Hershey store to buy a couple. Then very early on Christmas morning (5.30 am, if you don't mind), Steve and I crept into their hotel room to hang their stockings on their beds. We still do it every year, even at their age.

In the afternoon we went to the cinema. Steve and Charlie went to see the latest *Mission Impossible* film with Tom Cruise, but Emily and I didn't fancy that, so we went to see one called *The Darkest Hour*, which is about aliens invading Earth via our power supply. This turned out to be a massive mistake, as it was, without doubt, one of the worst films I've ever seen – absolute pants. The rest of the audience clearly agreed: not long into the film some people started to giggle, and it wasn't supposed to be a comedy! At the end of the movie, the man sitting in the next seat turned to me and said in a real New York twang, 'That truly was my darkest hour!'

'Well in England,' I said, 'that's what we call a load of bollocks!'

For our Christmas dinner we went to a great steakhouse that had been recommended to us called Uncle Jacks, in Midtown. It was a smart, old-style steakhouse with lots of dark wood, white linen tablecloths and red upholstery. Charlie said he had the best steak he's ever eaten, and even I tried red meat (a small piece of steak) for the first time in a year and quite enjoyed it. I think I'll still stick to fish or perhaps chicken in the future, but it was Christmas Day, so I thought, Why not? We had a fantastic time: very different from our usual Christmases, very different from our usual holidays, but wonderful nonetheless and an amazing end to the year.

Of course, as soon as you get home it's back to reality again. We arrived back in good old Blighty in the middle of fierce January storms to find a great big fallen tree blocking the lane leading to our house. Then, once we finally got inside, we discovered that a family of mice had been having a good old rave in our living room while we were away. Still, that's life, isn't it? And I guess I wouldn't want mine any other way.

So what's next for Pauline Quirke, I hear you cry! Well, we have distant plans to take the whole of August off and take the boat wherever we feel like going – just me, Steve and Bailey the dog. Before that, however, far from having a quiet life, the *Birds of a Feather* tour is looming. And yes, I'm still terrified; but as Charlie is going to have a part in it too, playing Sharon's son, I'll probably transpose some of my terror on to him, so my worries will either halve or double!

I'm certainly looking forward to it, though. Just like the last year and a half with *Emmerdale*, it marks the start of a whole new phase of my life, and, as per usual, I'm just going to try to take it in my stride. What else can you do? After all, at the end of the day, it's just a job – and that's something else this weird and wonderful year has taught me. Wherever my work takes me and whatever form it takes, I know that the most important thing to me is coming home afterwards to my family. On Mother's Day in 2011, Charlie wrote me a letter, which summed it up for me. I wasn't expecting it, I have to say, and I was pretty bowled over by it, especially coming from a 16-year-old of the male variety!

Dear Mum,
I'm just writing this letter to tell you how much I love you. I love you so much because of the laughs we all have together. Not many families I know can do that, and that's down to you. I respect you so much for what you have achieved,

but also for how gracious you are about being famous. Many children growing up have an idol, be it a footballer or a singer, etc. When I was younger, I thought mine was Ian Wright, but as I grow older I've now realized it is you, Mum. Not just because of your unbelievable acting abilities, but also the way you carry yourself: now a lighter mummy. I again respect you a crazy amount for sticking to LighterLife.

I'm so happy to see you losing weight, because you are now a happier person, and that makes me happy. I honestly hope that when I grow up, I will make you as proud of me as I am of you – if that's possible. You truly are an amazing person and I miss you when you're away, but I know you're doing it for us, so we can all go to New York!

Every time I see you on TV it makes me grateful to have such a great teacher in you, but also a great friend.

I love you Mum, don't ever change.

Charlie

A sense of achievement is always a good thing, whatever you decide to do in life: whether it's passing your driving test (yes, even on the fourth go), getting a good grade in an exam, or even just cooking a special meal that turns out beautifully, it's all good! But of the many things I've achieved in my own life and career, including the successes of 2011, my biggest achievement will always be my kids. And no job, however glamorous and exciting, can even come close to making me as happy as I am when I'm at home with Steve, Emily and Charlie. It's just the way I'm made, I guess!

There was one perfect night while we were in New York over Christmas. No, we weren't out at a fancy restaurant or a posh bar; we were just sitting in a hotel room. The four of us had walked our legs off that day, sightseeing and shopping, and by the time night fell we were just too tired to go out. We couldn't even be bothered to go downstairs and sit in a restaurant for an hour. So Emily, Steve and I trotted off to the nearest corner deli we could find and bought some drinks and sandwiches to bring back to the hotel room. We had such a fantastic time that night: eating overstuffed sandwiches together, talking nonsense and making one another laugh, with all of Manhattan buzzing below us. And for me it really hit home. Just the four of us in a room together . . . it's all you need really, isn't it?

Picture Acknowledgements

Section one

Page 3: PQ with Linda Robson and Lee Whitlock in *Shine on Harvey Moon* © ITV/Rex Features. Page 5: Linda Robson, Lesley Joseph and PQ in *Birds of a Feather* 'Maids of Ongar' (1998) and PQ, Lesley Joseph and Linda Robson in *Birds of a Feather* 'Ghost' (1998) both © FremantleMedia Ltd/Rex Features. Page 6: PQ and Linda Robson on *This Morning* (19 July 2011) and PQ, Linda Robson and

Lesley Joseph on *The Alan Titchmarsh Show* (11 October 2011) both © Steve Meddle/Rex Features.

Section two

Page 2: PQ, Peter Duncan and Linda Robson in *Dick Whittington* at the Hackney Empire (1991) © Rex Features. Page 4: PQ and cast of *Cold Blood* © ITV/Rex Features. Page 5: PQ standing behind Emmerdale sign and PQ outside the Woolpack Inn both © ITV Yorkshire Picture Archive. Page 6: PQ with Marc Silcock and Danny Miller © ITV/Rex Features; PQ at bar in the Woolpack Inn with Lucy Parteger and PQ on *Emmerdale* set wearing large cardigan both © ITV Yorkshire Picture Archive.

Section three

Page 4: Quirke family on *All Star Family Fortunes* © FremantleMedia Ltd. Page 6: PQ on LighterLife makeover shoot all images courtesy LighterLife. Page 7: PQ at British Soap Awards 2011 and TV Choice Awards 2011 both © Press Association Images.

Index

INDEX